Winning America to Christ

Jaroy Weber

BROADMAN PRESS
Nashville, Tennessee

© 1975 • Broadman Press
All rights reserved
4265-18
ISBN: 0-8054-6518-9

Library of Congress Catalog Card Number: 74-24668
Dewey Decimal Classification: 286
Printed in the United States of America

Winning America to Christ

Dedication

This book is dedicated to the messengers of the 1974 Southern Baptist Convention who expressed their confidence by electing me to serve as their president.

Foreword

This book is written to sound a note of hope in an hour of despair. I have recently traveled to almost every state in our union encouraging laymen, pastors, churches and denominations to "Win America to Christ." This is not to exclude the world, but we are all aware that God is doing certain miraculous works in other countries, works which are virtually absent from our country. To win the world we must first win America and commit all our spiritual and physical resources to the task of evangelism.

Evangelism must be church-centered to be effective and lasting. The method used must be in the church and out of the church to include personal and mass evangelism. I am convinced that the local church is the point of action. Every board, agency, commission, or cause is dependent on the local winning, calling out, and supporting of all worldwide efforts to reach men for Christ.

There are some basic emphases which need to be made in churches if revival is to come in power. I have listed several themes in these chapters which are basic and necessary in building a great church revival to win this world to Christ. There is no attempt to be scholarly or unique but rather an effort to sound again the fundamentals which seem to be utilized by God in building his Kingdom. The chapters are necessarily brief to provide space for numerous subjects which I feel are important.

Revival and renewal will affect the total life of our nation so that we will not relinquish our place of spiritual leadership in the world. To maintain our role in world missions we must have a revival of Christianity, in our land. This book is designed to restate those principles upon which our nation was built and call us back to our religious heritage.

Today we must win America to Christ—then in our redemptive role, we can win the world! We have the organizations, we have the resources. . . . our only need is REVIVAL!

Contents

1

Winning America to Christ

When I was elected president of the Southern Baptist Convention I quoted the remarks of President Gerald Ford when he stated, "This is one job I did not seek, but a responsibility I will not shirk." During my term of office I have two objectives in mind which have become a "magnificent obsession." The first is to honor Christ and the other is to help our great denomination. It is my prayer that both of these goals may have been achieved.

In fact, I personally feel that this is the motivation possessing all of us. We are different in our background, training, experience, and spiritual gifts, but together we constitute a perfect body of Jesus to continue doing what he came to do: "seek and save that which was lost." All our varied inputs to the body of Christ are of equal importance and significance, and no member can say to other members of the body, "I have no need of thee."

Our Convention theme is appropriate, "Let Christ's Freedom Ring." I am sure the committee had in mind the bicentennial celebration of our nation and our responsibility to proclaim true freedom in Jesus Christ. With this in mind, we must unite the birth of a nation to the need of a new birth in Christ.

We must use the historic significance of this time in history to become the tracks on which we can move in with the message of "good news" concerning Jesus Christ. Let's not permit civic organizations to take over the community celebration of our beginnings as a Christian nation while we remain silent on the sidelines. Let's run ahead of the crowd, leading the way in proclaiming that America was born in the fires of revival and has been sustained by revivals and has as her only moral or spiritual hope the revivals which come from our Father above.

America has been ripped apart by war, political corruption, crime, divorce, inflation, and recession. Now is the time to sound a note of hope and healing which comes from the gospel. Let us not remain silent, as a people of God, but speak the truth in love.

Why Win America to Christ?

While attending the World Congress of Evangelism, I heard Harold Lindsell, editor of *Christianity Today,* speak on "The Suicide of Man." In his message (also in *Christianity Today*) he declared several apparent evidences to his truth. He laid down the principle of the repetition of history, "In Noah's day suicide came as a result of man's rebellion to God." There are two ways man can commit suicide (1) by neglecting God's creation or a neglect of respect for the natural laws of God (2) by rejecting the Creator as fallen man has done in today's world.

Ecologically mankind is committing suicide. The great cities of the world such as Tokyo, London, and New York are being suffocated by smog from a materialistic industrial society. Our rivers and lakes are polluted, our cattle and vegetation killed by modern pesticides. The world is fast becoming an unsafe place in which to live.

Scientifically mankind is committing suicide. In the last several years we have tripled the knowledge of science until we have produced an "overkill." We have bombs, chemical germs, and other technological knowledge to annihilate all the human race in a few hours. We have produced pills to control our emotions, genetic balance, births . . . until we have a society living on pill therapy.

Morally mankind is committing suicide. In the name of freedom and reality our society has developed unprecedented display and circulation of pornography. Now sexual freedom is demonstrating itself in homosexuality, rape, sodomy, wife swapping, and unparalleled divorce. Many expressions of art, literature, and the theatre are so sex oriented as to destroy basic family life.

Sociologically mankind is committing suicide. The Roman Catholic Church has now attained the national average in divorce. Modern man in his unwillingness to make a spiritual commitment to Christ is unable to make a lasting commitment to another human being. A spirit of rebellion to all authority expresses itself in all age groups. The law is ignored; crime, alcohol, and drugs abound. "The great cities," as Francis Schaeffer writes, "are dying."

Intellectually mankind is committing suicide. There is a disregard for absolutes and all things have become relative under the persuasion of man's new reason. In all our newfound knowledge we have done as the book of Romans declared: we have not retained God in our knowledge (see Rom. 1:28).

What is happening to the world in general is happening to Western civilization in particular. Malcolm Muggeridge, a literary giant from England, said in *Christianity Today:*

> "I was reading the other day about a distasteful, but significant experiment conducted in some laboratory. A number of frogs were put into a bowl of water, and the water very gradually raised to boiling point, with the result that they all expired without making any serious effort to jump out of the bowl. The frogs are us, the water is our habitat, and the media, by accustoming us to the general deterioration of our values and our circumstances, ensure that boiling point comes on us unaware. It is my emphatic opinion that boiling point is upon us now, and that as a matter of urgency Christians must decide how they should conduct themselves in face of so apocalyptic a situation."

I am not willing to become a total pessimist because God is doing some great things in the world today. He is working through revival in some new areas, calling out a people for his name. I cannot be totally optimistic because I must face reality. Dr. J. W. Storer was quoted as saying: "In the light of what is happening I can't be an optimist or a pessimist but rather, I am a *hopist;* my hope is in Jesus Christ."

We can and must have hope for today! In spite of all that faces us we can and must win America!

This is a secular age and in the midst of it we are to proclaim the presence and the power of the spiritual. "The Kingdom of God is at hand" is the message for every believer to proclaim.

This is a secular age, and in the midst of it we are to sound forth the presence and the power of the spiritual. "The Kingdom of God is at hand" is the message for every believer to share.

This is an age when traditional religion is not so attractive to men. Against this background every Christian must witness to the reasonableness of the gospel. We must be able to give reason for the faith we hold in Jesus Christ.

This is an age of lostness. Man is in the grip of uncontrollable physical and social forces. Man is the slave of status, machines, economic systems, and fears. The worth of the individual seems lost. What a time to say: "God is love. God loves so much he sent Jesus Christ. God wants us to love him. God wants us to tell others that he loves them."

This is a selfish age expressing its selfishness in racism, nationalism, and isolationism. "All one man in Jesus Christ" (Gal. 3:28) needs to be proclaimed with joy.

How We Can Win America

It is rather simple but true, we must now use every available means to win every living person to Jesus Christ in our lifetime. The question which confronts us all is, What am I doing personally, what are we as an agency, commission, board, or institution doing to expedite this statement of truth?

As was pointed out earlier, 1976 is a significant moment in our American history, it has, however, some overtones and implications to our Baptist history. America was founded by men in search of religious freedom and in this freedom gained, was the fertile soil for our Baptist growth. Whether your historic position expresses itself in the "Trail of Blood" or the English Separatist movement, we must admit the contribution of men in America like John Clarke and others who gave impetus to our growth and development in Colonial struggle. As America has succeeded and grown, even so has our great group of people called Baptist. As our national population grew and people moved from the early colonial state, westward through the Allegheny passage until they covered the vast expanse even to the Pacific, Baptists were always there to be a force for God. We are part of this national empire and in a sense responsible for the good and bad which has resulted.

If we are a part of this society and it has become decadent and in need of repentance and revival, then we as a denomination, churches, or individual believers are in need of the same. Let us not insist that our nation is in need of a refreshing cleansing from God without being willing for ourselves to be cleansed. Then let us lead out, in godly example, to repentance and revival.

In our spirit of renewal we can make a total commitment of our persons and all our resources to achieve God's real purpose for us. It is now time for every church to reevaluate its church calendar and determine how every organization, every meeting, every worship experience validates the right to exist as God's expression of redemptive concern for fallen man. I would like for my church to be one of the first to say during this time: "Nothing is permitted in programming or budgeting that does not directly relate to the task of bringing men to God through Jesus Christ."

I have been convinced for a long while that every need of our fellowship is met within the incoming tide of evangelism. The local church is the point of action. When the local church fulfills its mission of reaching and making disciples, then other agencies, boards, commissions, and institutions are fed and maintained. Let the local church do anything but carry out the Great Commission and we are all out of business.

To accomplish what America needs, we must become more Baptist than ever before, yet we must be willing to join hands with any born-again believer, in local communities and around the world, in bringing the gospel to all men.

How then do we encourage the accomplishment of this? First of all, we can plan a Convention program that will develop an atmosphere and set a tone that is healing and helping. I have always prayed for the opportunity of attending a Convention meeting that is positive and yet provocative. Let the messengers leave with a tear of compassion rather than a trauma of tension. Why must we always leave with emphasis in our conflicts, disagreements, and debates? For once let's plan and produce the kind of program which will lead us to a personal sense of cleansing and renewal so that we can return to our various places of responsibility carrying a little fire from heaven. We all know that this is an annual business meeting, but why can't we have such a spirituality that lets us see we are all seeking the same objective of winning America in our lifetime?

Second, we can give evangelism the priority God gave to it. From a biblical perspective evangelism is God's priority. The church can and must perform many tasks, but evangelism makes the mission of the church Christian. This has been true in every age of the church's history since our Lord was here in the flesh.

Today there is ample evidence that God is uniquely at work through his spirit in the world. This work of God actually began in the last few months of the sixties and the first few months of the seventies. What happened was called the "Jesus Revolution." Out of this, suddenly some conditions were drastically and dramatically changed. Amazingly, the college campus, which had been closed to the gospel was wide open. Suddenly, lay people who had been refusing to make the sacrifices necessary to do the "work of the gospel" were willing to give all of Saturday as well as Sunday in "bus ministry." Our own denomination for three consecutive years passed the four hundred mark in baptisms.

God has given us an open door in evangelism. How long will this door remain open? Can we be sure that tomorrow will not bring another decade of rebellion and revolution? It is imperative that we do not commit the fatal mistake of merely making plans and then asking God to bless them. *We must go where God already has plans.* God is working in the midst of man's frustration and disillusionment.

As the largest group of evangelical Christians in the world, Southern Baptists have an obligation to put evangelism on the priority. We have the people, and we have the money. We *need* the desire and the commitment. We have done some things well. I mention the training of lay people for evangelism led by the Division of Evangelism. But we need to do our best! One evangelist maintains a network telecast of straightforward gospel preaching during the summer. Spring Street USA is on a number of TV stations. Campus Crusade can put six full time workers in one city to promote lay evangelism. Hundreds of our pastors are attending church administration seminars with a priority on evangelism conducted by interdenominational organizations because they want evangelism at the heart of everything we do.

The next two years are especially critical for evangelism because of several important factors:

1. The present conservative reaction has made people in general more open to the demands of the gospel.

2. It is in vogue (even popular) to talk about Jesus Christ. This is the time to put a heavy emphasis on witness training for every Christian.

3. The present secular atmosphere makes the gospel message of hope more needed. We need an evangelical and even evangelistic "theology of hope."

4. Our nation's approaching two hundredth birthday is rooted deep in evangelism. Woodrow Wilson declared in dedicating the Asbury Memorial, "America was born in a revival and back of the revival were the great preaches of the frontier." Many of our Baptist schools were begun by evangelists. What a time to return to the priority that made us great. A prominent British theologian said, "Southern Baptists preach the gospel and sing better than any people I know. I wish they would stick to doing what they do best."

In the light of all this there are definite commitments I would like to see Southern Baptists make. I would like to write across the years leading up to our two hundredth birthday as a nation the verse from Leviticus that is on the Liberty Bell in Independence Hall: "Proclaim liberty throughout the land unto all the inhabitants thereof."

1. I think every Southern Baptist and every Southern Baptist agency ought to support the plans of the Evangelism Division of the Home Mission Board for "Lifestyle Evangelism" in 1974-75 and "Proclamation '76" in 1975-76. I would like for every church to become involved in Lay Evangelism Schools, biblical renewal, and revivals. I would like for them to have the budget and staff help they need to lead our Convention to its greatest heights in evangelistic success.

2. I would like to see a renewal emphasis on evangelism in our Sunday Schools. We need to be inspired again to *find them, teach them, reach them, baptize them, and train them.*

3. I would like for us to have an emphasis on prayer. We can join in the "Prayer Lift '76" which will be led by the Evangelism Division and supported by WMU.

4. I would like to see us join our Sunday School organizations in challenging our people to read the Bible through during the year. Revivals have always been predicated upon a return to Bible reading. The Old Testament, New Testament, and present experiences validate this truth.

5. I would like for every one of us personally to witness in every wayside of our travels and in connection with our own church's program of witnessing. I ask that every member of my church staff be committed to personal evangelism. Every denominational leader ought to be a model for every pastor and every church member in personal witnessing. If evangelism is to be God's priority in our

lives it must not be just words but action.

6. I would like to call upon every board, every agency to put evangelism on a priority in their work. Everything we do is not evangelism, but we can make everything we do count for evangelism if this becomes our "magnificent motivation."

7. I would like to make the next two Convention meetings "celebrations of our life in Christ" with strong evangelistic motivations for our pastors and people. Most of the pastors hardly remember what they did in business sessions (except for a few controversial matters). They will never forget if we make these meetings "high hours" that point us to Christ and to a world that needs Christ.

8. I would like to see a special emphasis on evangelism in our seminaries during the next two years.

The Time to Win America Is Now

The evident urgency for the immediate is based on the biblical teaching of the imminent return of Jesus Christ. If the disciples believed he would come in their lifetime, so should we. Suppose we were told that we had only five years left to win America to Christ. What do you think would be the attitude of our denomination and churches? Would we rearrange schedules, give priority to funds, shelve the secondary, and be about our Father's business? We may have five years, five months, or five days. Jesus is coming!

This is the day of the resurgence of the common man. The common people always heard Jesus gladly. The rise of nationalism, the demonstration of labor unions demanding a more equitable share of goods, the march of the Women's Liberation Movement are all declarations that the common man is on the move. Now is the time to give meaning and purpose to his life, not through a new generation but through regeneration.

There is nothing that can stop us from marching across America, letting Christ's Freedom ring . . . but one thing. *The one hindrance and obstacle is a lack of concern.* We talk about priorities, plans, and proclamation and then go back to struggle with the secondary.

Sinclair Lewis was a great writer. Once an Italian editor came to interview Mr. Lewis after one of his speeches. He said, "Mr. Lewis, I have read your many books such as: *Babbitt*—which had to do with the American business man and his struggles and frustrations in a competitive society; *Elmer Gantry*—which was an exposure of the insincerity of some ministers; and *Main Street*—which discussed the problems of "little people in small towns. Mr. Lewis, I would like to ask you, do you have a solution to these problems?" The writer turned to the editor and said: "No, I do not have a solution to these problems and furthermore, I do not care."

The Italian editor later wrote: "Mr. Lewis is a great writer but he is not a great man. A great man not only knows the problem but he cares."

Actions speak louder than words. If we really care, God has given us the most strategic time in history to demonstrate it.

It is true, "This is no time to sit and cry but a time to do or die."

Proclamation of Liberty

Often we will meet a person whom we haven't seen for a long time and he will ask, "What's new?" Our reply then marks the beginning of a dialogue or conversation. There are many trends we consider new in the field of science, education, medicine, and even religion. We have new theologies, new social behavior in morality, and yet in Ecclesiastes we read, "There is no new thing under the sun."

July 4, Independence Day, a time when we celebrate our freedom and not only ours, but a new freedom for all peoples of the world. In every country, under every climate, out of every tribe, speaking every tongue, people are clamoring for freedom. This is nothing new. The Greeks were the first to envision a free society. Romans were the ones who developed highly a sense of law and justice for all men. As a matter of fact, Rome, the greatest empire the world has ever known, can be compared to our day.

There are four basic parallels which are apparent.

1. *Their system of law as compared to ours.* They developed a system of law based on fundamentals similiar to our laws.

2. *Sense of justice for all.* They gave the world the trial system, equality of all their citizens. The poorest of citizens could always appeal to Caesar, who was the same as our Supreme Court.

3. *Sense of freedom.* All the citizens were protected by the Roman Empire regardless of where they were. Paul illustrated this when enemies sought his life and he simply stated, "I am a Roman citizen," and they could not touch him. The entire force of Caesar's army gave support and protection to every citizen regardless of position. This was once true of an American citizen. The world knew that to endanger the life of an American citizen in any country would bring retaliation from our government.

4. *Capitalistic system.* They could own property, make a profit

in business, live in a structured class, for they had the rich, poor, and middle class.

5. *Basic freedom.* They had the basic freedom of religion, speech, and press. They could worship any god or no god, they could make speeches in the Forum, or write on any subject.

In spite of all these factors which resemble our systems of life they faced problems. They had law but inequalities under the law. They had social justice but slavery at its highest point in history. They had a capitalistic system, but immense poverty.

In the midst of this situation the Christian religion was injected into the blood stream of the Roman Empire. Did the Christians lash out at slavery? Did they condemn the social injustices of their day? Did they organize and promote a poverty program? Did they start crusades to break down color, class, and sex distinctions? It is evident that they did none of these. How did they relate their ministry to the problems of the world with such effectiveness that the Roman Empire adopted the Christian religion in less than three hundred years? The secret of their success was in this—the keynote of the Christian religion was freedom—but let us note the kind of freedom. To understand this let us go to the law and the testimony and see what Jesus spoke about it.

The Son of Man Shall Make You Free

Jesus, in denouncing the Jews, said to them, "If the Son therefore shall make you free, ye shall be free indeed" (John 8:36). To this they replied, "We are already free for we are Abraham's seed." Jesus likewise found this same response from the Romans for they considered themselves free citizens of the empire. Jesus knew that freedom based on the law was not real freedom. He advocated obedience to the law first, commanding that taxes be paid to the Roman government. He reminded the Jews that they were expected to obey the laws of Moses for Jesus had come not to destroy the law but to fulfill it. When he healed the lepers, he commanded them to go show themselves to the priest according to the law. The New Testament reflects the mind of Jesus in that we should never disobey the law but should be subject unto higher powers.

Two basic philosophies regarding the law are current in our land. This was expressed in the leadership of two prominent black leaders who have sought to lead their people in civil rights and freedom. Martin Luther King advocated that if one does not like the law, then he is to protest against it. Dr. J. H. Jackson preaches that one must abide by the law and work within the framework of the law to accomplish objectives. One must win the respect and recognition of the community in which he lives by being worthy of such trust.

Jesus considered all men as slaves to a master from whom he came to deliver us. In the New Testament the word "in" is used on five occasions to suggest "in bondage to." The statement is clearly descriptive of our enslavement to at least five masters which are listed.

1. In bondage to *sin*—Paul reminds us that we have all sinned and come short of the glory of God. This universal plague has blighted the total human race, and we are not able to overcome in our strength.

2. In bondage to the *law*—the law condemns us in our inability to keep the law. No man is perfect, no man can attain the high idealism of the Commandments and the related laws. The law binds us in our helplessness.

3. In bondage to the *flesh*—the New Testament implies that in every human there are two natures, good and evil. Paul pictures this constant warfare as a struggle, for when a man would do good he does evil. The evil, pride, or selfishness of human flesh can never be overcome by human strength.

4. In bondage to the *world system*—this is the spirit of self-centeredness. Even the religious leaders of Jesus' day, the Pharisees, were afflicted with this malady. When they prayed, they wanted it to be in public; and when they gave, they called attention to themselves by blowing trumpets. We are all alike in our egocentric spirits.

5. In bondage to *death*—this was man's last and worst enemy and no man was able to conquer death. Even the fear of death was impossible to conquer.

The Truth Shall Make You Free

Jesus is often referred to as the Word, the Way, and the Truth. In John 8:31 Jesus said, "If ye continue in my Word, then are ye my disciples indeed." The following verse reads, "And you shall know the truth and the truth shall make you free." In this context the "truth" is the Word of God. To know the Word, or observe the Word, is not the provision for liberty. One must do more; one must continue doing what the Word teaches. In James 1:25, we have the same usage, "But whoso looketh into the perfect law of liberty, and continueth therein," with emphasis on the word "continueth." We must do more than look, we must do. If we have been set free in redemption, we then follow after Christ as revealed in his Word. This indeed will set us free from self, envy, pride, hate, and all other vices incompatible with our Lord's life. This is the answer to world problems between nations, races, or capital and labor.

The Spirit Shall Make You Free

Paul says, "Now the Lord is that Spirit: and where the Spirit of the Lord is, there is liberty" (2 Cor. 3:17). With the Holy Spirit of God living in our hearts we have the power to do what we were unable to do before. Once we hated—now we love. Once we were selfish—now we are liberal. Once we were sensitive—now we can be abused for Christ's sake. Once we were weak—now are we strong. Now you can treat your enemies better than they deserve because that is the way God treats you.

Now we understand what the New Testament means by there being neither rich or poor, good or bad, cultured or uncultured, black or white, but we are all *one in Christ.* The United Nations can't make us that way. The political system can't make us that way. The church can't make us that way. Jesus Christ alone can make us one in his fellowship of saints.

When will this idea of freedom dawn upon our country? When will it dawn upon Africa, Asia, Russia, and all nations of the earth? Our world has worked at this problem for over two thousand years and failed, but the Roman Empire saturated with Christianity solved it in three hundred years. This is the liberty we must universally proclaim to all men, then they will be free indeed.

In spite of all the freedom the Romans claimed, they were slaves to the masters of their lives. None of them could say that he had the power to overcome sin, law, flesh, world system, or death. Jesus says, "Here is the freedom you need and only I can give it to you." He was to do this not with law but the gospel.

Jesus was to make this freedom possible through what we know as redemption. This is a dramatic word which is a description of what God in Christ does for us in salvation. Adolph Deitzman in one of his books tells how the freedom of slaves was purchased in the time of Roman power. Often during an auction someone would step from the crowd and purchase a slave from the auction block and say, "In the name of god, I set you free." From this point on the slave was free to go and do what he pleased. Only one commitment was necessary—he must worship and serve the god in whose name he had been delivered. Paul uses this picture to declare that we are not our own, we have been bought with a price." We are not redeemed with corruptible things such as silver and gold, but with the precious blood of Christ. Being redeemed with his blood, the only demand is that we confess him and serve him. He has given us a new freedom!

3

A Look at the World

Jesus challenged, "Lift up your eyes and look upon the field" [world] (John 4:35). We view a vastly changed world but the basic need is the same . . . Jesus. The fact that distinguishes our day from previous times is obviously our mastery over the scientific means of life and not the spiritual.

We can recall through the pages of history the crude, backward manner in which our forefathers lived. We have witnessed by experience the modern changes of today and know that we have come a long distance in scientific progress. There was a day when the fastest mode of transportation was on foot or by donkey. Now one can travel thousands of miles a day and think nothing of it. The first locomotive train—invented by a Frenchman, Nicholas Cagnot—was exhibited in 1763. It was more a self-moving steam engine which was to run on common roads. It had a speed of less than four miles per hour and stopped every fifteen minutes to build up the steam pressure. While running the engine at a speed of three miles per hour, it overturned. The public authorities, who considered it dangerous and a menace to public safety, ordered it locked up.

When the Wright brothers dreamed that a machine with wings could fly through the air, they were laughed at and ridiculed. One of their fellow citizens remarked, "No one will ever fly, and if they do, it will not be someone from Dayton, Ohio." Today planes can fly around the world without refueling. Space ships may one day soon be running excursions to the moon.

Yesterday friends could live within a few miles of each other and never get acquainted . . . now with modern television, radio, and telephone it can be done by remote control. Not many years ago only a few people could own a telephone and then not without several regular listeners on the party line. Now telephones are often installed in automobiles, and while a wife is stopped at a traffic light, she can call her husband to give final instructions on how to take care of the baby!

In past days all that man ate was produced by his hands and prepared in the crudest way. Soon one will be able to rise, dress for work, and en route to the job take a pill which will include enough vitamins and nutrition to carry him until noon when he will take two more pills.

In the days of Greek history, thousands of Greek soldiers with shields and spears would go into battle with about as much struggle and blood as a football game. Many times in battle with thousands engaged, only a few would be injured and fewer killed. Today one nuclear bomb can destroy a city and if made large enough could destroy all the inhabitants of the earth.

Lift Up Your Eyes

As we lift up our eyes to view the world, we cannot escape the scene of a broken world. We are broken politically, socially, and morally to such a degree that only the Lord can bind us up and heal us.

About every quarter of a century, we bathe our world in the warm blood of war which is evidence that we are broken internationally. Nations cannot agree upon any Christian standard which will usher peace into our troubled world. As we talk about peace, every major nation is preparing, in a measure, for the possibility of war in the immediate or near future. We are broken internationally and will always be until the same Christ who conquered the Roman Empire in three generations conquers the materialistic nations of the world, not excluding America.

Not only is there trouble internationally but nationally. Government cliques that attempt to destroy each other, a death struggle between capital and labor, racial problems causing violence, and other problems are eternal dicta to the truth . . . we are broken politically. Congresses, parliaments, legislatures, and politics have failed to answer man's basic need . . . regeneration.

We are broken socially. Conduct which would have brought condemnation from decent society yesterday, is now fashionable, acceptable, the thing to do! God has not changed his standards, we have changed our convictions. The Bible has been replaced in many

American homes by *Playboy, Playgirl,* and *Cosmopolitan.* Old time convictions which were as true as sixteen ounces to a pound, twelve inches in a foot, and four quarts in a gallon, have been lost in the mad rush of multiplication, elaboration, and accumulation of the means of life while the ends of life are forgotten. Such is illustrated by the man found dead in his New York apartment. A note left by his bedside read, "Too darn much money."

We are broken morally. American homes end up in the divorce courts at the rate of two out of five. In one Texas county alone within one year there were more divorces granted than marriage licenses. Dr. Vance Havner observed: "We will never have a revival until families wear out more carpets around the family altar than around the dressing tables. When fathers stay home from the club and mothers from their parties and children from their dances and the car is left in the garage long enough to cool and the radio is shut off long enough to tune in on God . . . we will have a revival and not before." A radio commentator remarked recently, "What America needs is six-million homes." We did not realize how much truth was involved in that statement. America does need six-million homes where God is the silent partner in every affair, where children are taught respect and honor, where parents are in love with each other.

We lift up our eyes to see a hungry world. Have you ever been hungry? In all probability you have never been on the verge of starvation. It is most difficult for us to perceive how people could starve in a land of plenty. During the recent food conference in Rome it was indicated that there are nations of this world that will starve because of a lack of food. You can stand on a street corner of a great city in India about five o'clock in the morning and see large garbage trucks rolling down silent streets. They are not picking up garbage, but the dead who have starved during the night. In some countries, schools have been converted into hospitals to care for those who are sick with malnutrition. In large cities this winter, little children will eat their best meals from waste cans. We do face a hungry world.

More eager than a starving man for food, a perishing man for water, a dying man for his mother, are the people of the world for salvation. They cannot express it in theological terminology, but they are hungry for God and peace through Jesus Christ.

One can envision the multitudes on every far-flung continent of the globe. The desperate, humiliated, brow-beaten, despondent people of Japan; the tired weary, longing throngs of China; the superstitious clans of Africa—are all hungry for the gospel. But we must not overlook our need at home. In almost every American home people are lost. A wife, husband, son, daughter, or others who are as lost as the heathen who have never heard the gospel. In my experience as a soul-winner, I have always observed that most people are anxious and hungry for the way that leads home to God . . . the cross of Calvary!

Gird Up Thy Loins

In biblical days the garment of apparel was a long rectangular strip of cloth. It was wound around the body and then draped by the side. This type of garb impeded speed, so when a race was to be run or a battle fought, the long flowing garment was gathered and placed beneath the belt to avoid entanglement. Paul used this figure to illustrate the necessity of spiritual alertness.

This implies several thoughts: First, it indicates haste because of brevity of life. Pick up your newspaper and what do you read? A great passenger plane flying into an airport collides with another plane, killing fifty-five and seriously injuring the pilot! A mighty ship sinks with several hundred on board! The floods of China! The earthquake in Central America! The plague of disease taking more lives than wars! All this is a warning of the brevity of life.

The second coming of Jesus Christ is another reason for us to make haste. The Scripture clearly states: "Watch therefore, for ye know neither the day nor the hour wherein the Son of man cometh" (Matt. 25:13). Because he could come today, tomorrow, or in a thousand years, we ought to try and win as many to Christ as we can before it is too late.

There is no sadder picture than for mother or father waiting too late to win their children, or a friend his friend, or a stranger the stranger. It was tragic when the people tried to get into the ark after Noah and his family were in but found it impossible. More tragic than that . . . when Christ comes and we have failed to win those about us.

It is indicative of an urgent necessity. Our number one need of today is compassion. We do not really believe that people are lost. Vague is the conception in our minds of the condition of people outside the kingdom of God, and we do not fully comprehend that people are lost and that their destiny is an eternal, everlasting hell separated from God forever and forever.

Jesus stood on the hill overlooking Jerusalem and wept because he had compassion on the people. Oh! I would that we could have his compassion! That it could be said of us like it was said of John Wesley, "He was out of breath pursuing souls." We should have and manifest the passion for souls which Whitefield had when he testified: "I am willing to go to prison and to death for you, but I am not willing to go to heaven without you."

We need the passion that girded Francis Asbury as he traveled a distance equal to five circuits around the world every five years, on the average, for forty-five years—and that mainly on horseback. We need the passion that stirred Livingston and kept him aflame amid jungle dangers and twenty-seven attacks of African fever. We need the passion working in the heart of David Brainerd who said, "I care not what hardships I endure, if only I can see souls saved." The passion that drove Moody to witness to at least one soul a day, the passion that drives our noble, God-called preachers to work, visit, and witness fifteen to eighteen hours a day. This is our need, oh, God!

Such ought to be our compassion and concern until we would be like the man whose wife was ill. She was in the hospital where the doctors and nurses were tending to her while the anxious husband walked the floor. He stopped and asked the doctor, "Is there anything I can do, Doctor?" "No," replied the doctor, "We are doing all that can be done." Several times he did this until finally he cried, "Doctor, I think I'll die if I can't do something for my wife." Only until we have a similar concern for the lost will we win them to Christ.

Likewise, this Scripture passage is indicative that we "stand in the need of prayer." Before we can ever hope to reach for Christ, we must tarry in prayer. We must pray until every known sin is forgiven. We must pray until we see the terrible condition of a lost world, until we see men, women, precious children sinking into

eternal hell. We must pray until we have compassion. We must
pray until God gives us a message. We must pray until power is
ours . . . then go! We must pray as John Knox prayed, "Oh, God,
give me Scotland or I die." God give me my son, daughter, husband,
wife, friend, enemy, and stranger. Such is the kind of praying that
assures victory.

It is also indicative of a battle. Not all will remain faithful as
we go into the battle of soul-winning. The time will never come
when we can count on every man to join the ranks, but we have
enough men in our churches and communities to start a revival in
our cities and states which could turn the world upside down for
God.

Take Up Thy Cross

Hindrances are involved as we seek to take up our cross. The
most subtle hindrance to a Christian is the plague of preoccupation.
It is not that the Christian is objecting to God's will for his life;
it is only that he is already so busy with incidentals that he cannot
do the main thing.

This story is told by Dr. Melton from Texas: As a boy my family
lived in the country where my father ran a small grocery store.
Two prominent men in the community became involved in a feud
and threatened each other. One day one of the men came to my
father's store, carrying a gun. My father asked him where he was
going, and he said, I am going to kill my neighbor before he kills
me. My father finally whispered in my ear and told me to run as
fast as I could through the field to the home of this man and warn
him of the trouble. I never shall forget that trip—through the corn
and cotton fields I ran as fast as a boy could. Finally, I came to
a wooded area and decided I would rest. In the meanwhile I grew
interested in the birds and started throwing rocks at them. I knocked
one down, picked him up and played for a while and started on
my way. When I arrived at the farmer's house I noticed a great
crowd of people about and upon inquiring I was told that our
neighbor had been killed. As fast as my bare feet could fly, I hurried
back to my father's store. As he looked me over, his eyes fell on
my hands. Said he, 'Son, what is that on your hands?' I replied,
'Father, that is the blood of a bird I killed.' 'No, son,' Father replied,
'That is the blood of a man whom you failed to warn because you

played on the way.' "

At the judgment our Savior will look upon our hands and say, "Mother, what is that on your hands? The blood of your daughter whom you failed to win to Christ." "Father, what is that on your hands? The blood of your son whom you failed to win to Christ." "Preacher, what is that on your hands? The blood of souls you failed to win to Christ." What an indictment against any Christian!

Another hindrance to the Christian is presumptuous sin. The out and out sin in the life of the Christian robs him of spiritual concern for the lost. As we search our lives, we find present attitudes, desires, and habits that serve as a hindrance to God's using us as an instrument of power.

This command of our Savior to take up our cross is to be heeded by every Christian. God has a plan for winning the lost of every community . . . personal evangelism resulting in mass evangelism. Jesus was a personal soul-winner. The Gospels present nineteen different times when he sat down to win and teach one individual. The disciples were personal soul-winners as they talked to people individually. Effective evangelists have been men who believed in and practiced soul-winning.

After World War I, one of our submarines sank in the Atlantic Ocean. As they were going down, they sent out an SOS message asking for help. All of the aids for rescue were made available. The submarine was soon located by a deep-sea diver going down from a sister ship. The sailor knew that he could not rescue the men, seventy-two strong, by opening the hatchdoor so he began to make inquiry through morse code. He tapped on the side of the ship, which being interpreted read, "Are you there?" As quick as a flash the code replied, "We are all here." Without hesitation the men asked, "Is there any hope?" The sailor, trying to comfort them replied, "Yes, there is hope." With nervous tension and a spirit of suspense the trapped men cried: "If there is hope then how long will it be? How long will it be?"

This lost world is asking if there is any hope, and we all are quick to reply that there is definite hope. But the question they continue to ask, "How long will it be?" I must reply that it will be as long as it requires Christians to receive a glimpse of the lost world and take up their cross *to do something about it. You* have the answer to their cry!

The Genius of Denominational Growth

Religious surveys indicate that many denominations are declining while a few are continuing to grow. The thesis of this chapter is to discover the cause of decline and also the cause of growth and make applications that are appropriate. I am pleased that our denomination is included in the denominations that are growing. To properly evaluate the present, we must review the past.

A point of humor is seen in the story of the governor who visited the mental institution in his state. While on the premises he tried to place a telephone call to the outside. The operator was delayed in immediately securing the number, and the delay irritated the governor. In impatience he screamed to her, "Young lady, you do not know who I am, do you?" "Smiling" over the phone, the young lady calmly replied, "No, I do not know who you are, but I know *where* you are".

Conception

There are two basic theories concerning our Baptist origin. All of us subscribe to one of these or a combination of both. It is not my purpose to prove either point but to survey the theories.

The first is that of *historical succession;* that is, that we are an extension of the original New Testament organization. Historians relate this theory to the idea that we see our historic beginning in the John-Jordan concept and that John was baptizing in our faith. The other phase of historical succession is the "spiritual kinship" theory; whereby, we were not in the beginning by name but in nature of our conformity to New Testament practices. According to this view, our history parades itself through many groups of sects under different names and finally evolves as Baptist.

The other major theory is that of the English Separatist. During the seventeenth century a group separated themselves from the state church of England and under John Smyth went to Holland where in 1607 they organized the first independent group. This group later left Smyth and followed Murton and Helwys back to Spittlefield, London, where they organized the first Baptist group in 1611.

The truth of the whole matter is that our validity is more dependent on our present practice of New Testament teachings than our pedigree. One can hardly account for the tremendous growth of the early church except in a threefold manner. First, there was the belief in spiritual gifts which included a divine call and purpose. Second, the early church believed in the immediate return of Christ which gave the members a sense of urgency. Third, they knew that God had pointed them to a destiny and would direct them through it.

Our Baptist heritage in America is often connected with Roger Williams, who indeed was not a Baptist in the strict sense, having later gone with the "Seekers." Perhaps we are better represented in John Clarke of Newport, Rhode Island, who organized a Baptist church in 1644. From this infant beginning, we grew to our first association in 1707, to the Triennial Convention in 1813, and to the Southern Baptist Convention in 1845.

Conflict

As have all other denominations, we have had our problems and conflicts. In 1845 we saw Baptists split over the slavery issue. Baptists from the South then formed the Southern Baptist Convention. We did not travel far until trouble developed within our camp in the form of the anti-mission campaign under the leadership of Daniel Parker, Joshua Lawrence, Alexander Campbell, and others. Hardly had the wound healed until fresh revolt appeared in the form of "Landmarkism," led by J. R. Graves and J. M. Pendleton. The miracle is that the spirit and purpose of our original convention continued to live and grow while these splinters died. In a growing organism we will always have conflict, but my prayer is that its result will be for the furtherance of the gospel.

Some of our basic conflicts have appeared in the area of social upheavals, mainly the race issue. The Supreme Court forced many denominations, including ours, to face more realistically the unchristian attitude of many people. The Christian Life Commission was courageous enough to sound the trumpet again and again until many of us heeded the biblical truth concerning the equality of all men.

Time has proven that there was not so much a desire to integrate churches as a desire to maintain human dignity and have the same rights as all other human beings. Many Christians, even though unaware of it, have helped give black people a new sense of pride within their own race. At present, many white churches have lowered barriers to encourage entrance by all people.

Another crisis occurred—which was theological—over Professor Ralph H. Elliott's book, *The Message of Genesis*. After considerable debate a committee headed by Dr. H. H. Hobbs was given the task of preparing a new statement of "Baptist Faith and Message." This move quieted the troubled waters and the statement was adopted at the Convention meeting in Kansas City in June, 1963.

Another crisis of importance was centered around the Sunday School Board's *The Broadman Bible Commentary*. There was a strong opposition to some passages and events interpreted by the author of Volume 1. At the Denver Convention meeting of 1970 the Convention asked the Board to remove this volume from distribution and select another writer to approach the Genesis account from the conservative position.

We have faced our conflicts and controversies, but our democratic and autonomous fellowship permits self-cleansing and change to accommodate our convictions.

Contributions

While others stand amazed at our ability to progress amid conflict, we have not been lacking in contributions to the religious life of the world.

These are not listed in order of importance, but note our emphasis on "soul competency" as preached by E. Y. Mullins. Soul competency does not mean that man is competent in self or that the innate goodness of man demands the consideration of God. Competency is every man's right to stand before God as a sinner and ask for forgiveness of sin without human intervention.

Our concept of the church is of prime consideration. First, we believe that there must be a regenerate membership voluntarily baptized by immersion. The church is a local autonomy whose main business is evangelizing the whole world.

Today as never before we are proud of our Virginia Baptists who were persistent in demanding that the Constitution make clear the matter of separation of church and state. Three concepts capture the thinking of world leaders in relationship to church and state. Some religious groups advocate that the church control the state, since the spiritual is superior to the material. Others advocate that the state preserve the church; thus the state must be in control. The third concept is that of the Baptists, a free church existing in a free state, both respecting the freedom of the other.

Some have emphasized that our greatest contribution has been our doctrine of the lordship of Jesus Christ. This truth makes possible and secures our salvation. It determines the nature and mission of our churches. It likewise promises us a final triumph of the kingdom of God.

We have made significant contributions in the area of evangelism. One could not soon forget our leadership in simultaneous revivals by C. E. Matthews, our city-wide revivals by C. E. Autrey, and our personal evangelism by Kenneth Chafin in the "Win" materials. These concepts have not only been tools for us but have served as avenues whereby we can join hands with all other evangelicals in winning people to Christ. All of us would immediately express our appreciation for materials and programs contributed by other denominations and independent groups to our work.

Cause of Growth

Fundamental is the fact that we have kept the Bible central. We must never make the Bible an end in itself but the truth toward which it points us is important. The Bible is not just another book but an instrument which points us to our sickness and God's remedy. It is not the "Book of the Month" but of eternity.

In our frontier expansion, old preachers told great Bible stories which struck a familiar note in the minds of the people—and the people responded. This book does not need us to defend it with theological arguments but to preach its simple message of salvation.

Baptists have always believed in the importance of preaching the gospel with the result of changing the hearts of men. John Taylor and other pioneer preachers mounted their horses and rode out to the camps to preach. They knew little of theology but much of the power of God to save.

Baptists have always had an adaptability to any situation, thus staying close to the people. Perhaps the Methodist circuit rider was not as effective as the pioneer Baptist preacher because the circuit rider came through preaching but the Baptists lived with the people, plowing during the week and preaching on Sunday. This has kept us in touch with the needs of the masses and has adapted our message and program to the particular needs of the community. In America many Protestant churches have settled in the class of the economically comfortable. Baptists have had the same message, but an adaptability in approach in every group from the brush-arbor to the cathedral. Freedom of belief, expression, and experimentation gives us the genius of staying close to the people.

One secret of our growth is plain hard work. We are reminded of our pioneer forefathers like Williams, Clarke, Holmes, and others, who paved the way for us in their blood. Our hard work has kept us from majoring on minors. We have left the debate up to Alexander Campbell and theological hair-splitting to other groups while we have moved out in an effort to evangelize and educate.

Consequences

Along with our tremendous growth has come many natural consequences. First, there is a tendency in some areas to do as other large denominations—to institutionalize our religion by drawing in our stakes from new areas and building large institutions in established areas.

Some years ago in *The Quarterly Review*, there was a discussion concerning the ministerial students' concept of the ministry as big business. Too many have felt the smaller churches were but stepping-stones to larger work and the whole concept was businesslike. Any God-called preacher who is serving any Baptist church is in the biggest business in the world!

We have been swept off our feet by the trends of psychology. Too many of us are trying to get out of our field and to psychoanalyze our people, when all many of them need is a sense of sins forgiven. Let us understand the problem but leave the field to Norman Vincent Peale and others.

For a while we were obsessed with a desire to innovate to become relevant. Much of this innovation deleted an emphasis of basic and fundamental principles of Bible study and personal evangelism, so numbers of churches died. Only those groups who remained with the New Testament principles of outreach survived this struggle for survival.

Our darkest day will come if we settle down in a middle-class group and forget the multitudes who are down and out or up and out. We cannot leave the economically oppressed to the sects of America or the wealthy to the stately churches of our day. Our message and ministry is the same to all groups who are in need of our Savior.

There is a consensus on the part of a very few that we must join the ecumenical movement which has been a fad of the mid-twentieth century. There was much pressure exerted for me to sign the Lausanne Covenant and even though I could agree with the contents I did not feel that Southern Baptists would want me to involve them in a theological statement. We love Billy Graham and respect his ministry and will join hands with all evangelicals in missions and evangelism. I feel sure that as long as Baptists do as well, under God's leadership, as we are now doing, and we have men who have the evangelistic spirit as we do, there is no fear of our loss of identity in this amalgamation of denominations.

It is a good omen to find Baptists stressing the need of education. In fact we have been slow in this emphasis. It is a thrill to see our seminaries with record enrollments. The Baptist preacher must be educated in order to have contact with the modern world. However, we must not permit our evangelistic spirit to abate with educational preoccupation. We do not have to have one or the other *but both together.*

Caution

Caution lights blink ahead as we face the future and wisdom has fled from us if we ignore them. There are two emphases today: one is to preserve the past and the other is to change in order to make the churches relevant for today. Our democratic spirit permits enough elasticity in belief that we can work these two together for the expansion of our work.

With the growth of our Southern Baptist Convention, it has become impossible to transact all business from the floor of the Convention—thus more and more committees are caring for these needs. We must remember the adage of B. H. Carroll, "Tell the people and trust the Lord." We must recognize in our mass organization the need for all our pastors, denominational leaders, and educators to have a voice in our work. While we maintain our growing organization, let us never stop the man who gives constructive criticism, for such a man keeps us from being bureaucratic. Human nature will prevent us from having a faultless organization. Every effort must be made to preserve unity among Southern Baptists. There is a difference of opinion among Baptists of the East and West, North and South and such will be true as long as we expand into new territory where there is a new culture. The spirit of democracy, however, gives us this freedom of difference yet unity.

Perhaps one of the most emotional decisions we have faced is the name change of the Southern Baptist Convention. Any intelligent person readily recognizes advantages and disadvantages involved. I have always had the faith to believe that we are mature enough to give careful study to a situation, vote our convictions, and abide by the majority decision. Our attitude toward the voice of the Convention is more important than the problems we sought to resolve. We are not divided. E. S. James' statement is true, "Southern Baptists are kept together by a commitment to the resurrection and evangelism."

As we face the future, we are not bound with a creed which crystalizes all we can believe. For Baptists it is every man before God with an open mind and an open Bible. Let us always be willing to reexamine our doctrine in the light of New Testament teaching.

> Lead on, O King Eternal! The day of march has come;
> Henceforth in fields of conquest Thy tents shall be our home.
> Through days of preparation Thy grace has made us strong,
> And now, O King Eternal, We lift our battle song.
>
> Lead on, O King Eternal, We follow not with fears;
> For gladness breaks like morning Wher'er thy face appears,
> Thy cross is lifted o'er us; We journey in the light:
> The crown awaits the conquest; Lead on, O God of might.

5

Evangelize Now

Dr. Harold Ockenga replied to a six page report of the *U.S. News and World Report* that stated the churches were in trouble. Dr. Ockenga replied the churches are in trouble with their theology, their moral teaching, their social action, their preoccupation with politics, their ecumenical stance, and their evangelism of involvement.

If one does not agree with the statement of the above, all he needs do is read Roger Shinn's *Tangled World* or Harvey Cox's *Secular City* or Joseph Fletcher's *Situation Ethics*. We are in trouble, because we have failed to fulfill the biblical mission of the church—to evangelize.

The word *evangelism* is not found in the New Testament; however, the word for *evangelize* is used fifty-two times, and the noun form of good news or "gospel" is used seventy-four times. We must now define evangelism so that we may recast our responsibility to modern man. Some speak:

D. T. Niles: "Evangelism is one begger telling another begger where to find bread."

Leighton Ford: "Evangelism is a cross in the heart of God."

Archbishop's Committee on Evangelism in 1918 stated: "Evangelize is so to present Christ Jesus in the power of the Holy Spirit, that men shall come to put their trust in God through Him, to accept Him as their Saviour and serve Him as their king in the fellowship of His Church."

Evangelism needs more than a mere definition, it needs a demonstration. Then it becomes:

The cry of John Knox—"Give me Scotland or I die."

The vision of John Wesley—"The world is my parish."

The commitment of Henry Martyn, landing on the shores of India, crying, "Here let me burn out for God."

The sacrifice of Brainerd, coughing up blood from his tubercular lungs as he prays in the snow for the Indians.

The spirit of Jim Elliot and his young friends who stained the sands of a bitter river in Equador as they died to evangelize the Auca Indians.

The dedication and sacrifice of Bill Wallace who "lived himself to death" in reaching the lost in China.

The statement of Archbishop Temple is correct, "The Church is the only organization in the world which does not exist for its members."

We have tried to evangelize without commitment, but as Dr. Johannes Schneider has stated, "Evangelism without commitment is no evangelism at all, but only a kind of religious activity."

We will never evangelize until we take seriously the commission of Jesus—"Go ye unto all the world and preach the gospel to every creature."

Let us note first what he meant by this statement.

Condition of the World_"All the World"

It is a big world.

Almost four billion people live on the face of the earth with 208,000 babies born every minute. More than two billion people live where there are no Christians and over one billion has never heard the gospel. With the scientific development of radio, television, and Telstar, we could reach every corner of the universe in less than eight minutes, but we are getting the "good news" out at a slower rate than our forefathers in oxcarts.

It is a confused world.

Man is confused as to his identity. Who is he, this modern man? Is he a mere accident, a product of evolution, a pebble on a planet, or a human being divinely created in the image of God? Man doesn't know for sure. He is confused as to his identity. He is spiritually sick, and as John Baillie says in *A Sense of the Presence of God,* "Man is not whole or healthy." He expresses it like Rabbi Liebman who wrote a leading book on peace of mind, then committed suicide.

Man is in considerable doubt as to his ultimate destiny. Why was I born? Why am I here? What do I want in life? Where am I going? In short, what is my destiny? Man doesn't know. He is like Christopher Columbus on his westward journey—he didn't know where he was going, where he was, or where he had been. Space-age man is like that. He, too, doesn't know where he is going, but tomorrow approaches and he must do something or go somewhere, but what to do and where to go—he doesn't know.

Man is fearful and depressed about survival. He feels his need to survive as a member of society, but atomic bombs stare him in the face if he does survive.

Oh! but for a voice from the wilderness of asphalt, brick, and steel, saying "For God so loved the world, that he gave his only begotten Son."

It is a lost world.

We speak of modern man today with such sophistication that we forget that God sees him as fallen man. University uprisings, advanced education, race marches, Social Security enlargement, and even the ending of American involvement in the war in Vietnam have not overcome men's lostness.

"Too often we try to meet man's problem by recasting the gospel rather than converting the sinner," Carl Henry says. Man doesn't know he is fallen and must be told about it.

Man's lostness is personalized and expressed in war, crime, lust, hate, and other abnormalities of nature. It is more personally seen in the following:

Emptiness—The famous Swiss psychologist Jung has stated that the central neurosis of our time is emptiness and meaninglessness. This is daily reflected in art, music, philosophy, and literature. When intelligent Americans line up for four city blocks to see *Who's Afraid of Virginia Woolf?* where God's name is used in vain forty-two times and obscene language is the topic of conversation, and when *The Exorcist* in which Satan is the star and the most vile language and activity is reproduced on the screen, is held over for months all across the nation by popular demand, it must speak of man's plight.

Loneliness—It is one thing to be lonely for friend or family, but there is an "existential loneliness" which appears in the enjoyment of human accomplishment and company. This loneliness is the absence of God in life. Regardless of man's progress, material gain, or old age security, man can never be at peace with himself or God until Jesus Christ comes to live in his life.

Guilt—Most of man's emotional problems and many of his organic illnesses are due to his inability to deal with guilt. Psychiatric treatment, anti-depression pills, or a new book on peace of mind can never remove the stain of guilt. The Bible is true, "Behold the Lamb of God, which taketh away the sin of the world."

Fear of Death—The attempt of man to escape the reality of death is seen in his attempt to remain youthful, his attack on funerals, his resolve that death will not be mentioned. The theologian Helmut Thielicke has stated, "Death is coming to have the same position in modern life and literature that sex had in the Victorian times." The Bible declares that God created man to live and not to die but sin entered in and changed God's plan. The Christian gospel restores God's initial plan for man and defeats his last enemy, death. We cannot escape—let us face it.

The Commission to the World

This commission is still to the church in today's world. Paul's concept of the church was that the church is located in a hostile environment as a little colony of heaven. One writer compares the church to the early American Colonies living behind the walls of a stockade and venturing out in the day but retreating back to the stockade at night. The church must become involved, it must penetrate society, it must speak a message of hope to the hopeless. The story is told of a Chinese boy who came to America to study. He failed his courses and was found hiding in a church attic, crouched in shame, afraid to face the world. This is often the picture of the church—hiding in the four walls of the church, afraid to face an educated, lost world. How is this involvement to be accomplished? Jesus has given us the direction in his commission—the Great Commission:

1. It included an announcement, "All authority in heaven and on earth has been given me."

Jesus declares this of himself only after his resurrection. This means that even though the devil is the "prince of this world," God is still in charge of history. He has authority over believers, all of us, and commands, "As my Father hath sent me, even so send I you—go!" We can do no less than he commands since he is in authority. He is over the unbeliever and gives him the option of receiving or rejecting him. The key is in our hands for he declares, "I give you the keys of the kingdom" or the gospel; and if you declare it, men will be loosed from their imprisonment to sin and self. If you fail to evangelize, men will remain lost.

He is given authority in heaven so that no power or demon can change his compassion and capability of redemption for men.

2. It includes direction: "Go ye." His commission as stated in John 20:21 says: "As my Father hath sent me, even so send I you." Go. This is an imperative and must be obeyed, for failure to follow his command is not just neglect, it is treason. The church's mission then is to be like Christ. Jesus was the first missionary evangelist, and he has given us the direction to follow. His mission—

—Involved birth into the world. Jesus didn't stay in heaven and issue orders but rather laid aside his glory and became involved. To put it another way, he did not throw a lifeline to the drowning man but rather jumped in with him.

—Involved life in the world. "He dwelt among us." "The Word was made flesh." Jesus was critized for his personal involvement with sinners, but there was no other way to reach human need than to sit where men sat. The church cannot exist behind the walls of a monastery but must be thrust into the bustle of the marketplace. Jesus lived in a secular society to win sinners. How many sinner friends do you have?

—Involved death for the world. Jesus not only took upon himself our nature but our sins. He was "made flesh" but also "made sin for us." Jesus then died for us, and we can do no less for sinners than he did. When the church reaches this passion which supercedes our desire for church success, denominational approval, or personal accomplishment, then people will be won to Christ.

3. A promise is declared: "And, lo, I am with you."

Jesus promised, after his resurrection, to be with his disciples. This he still does individually, when two or three are gathered in his name, or many meet in worship. He also declares his presence when they are going! He now stands at the right hand of the Father to make intercession for sinners, but he also abides with us in the Holy Spirit. He is working to convict of sin, righteousness, and judgment. He only needs our willingness to be channels through which he can work to bring good news of hope to sinners. He will be with us in perils, problems, persecutions.

Conquest of the World

Theologians have talked about the end of the age or world as we now understand it without finding much hearing, but there is a new scientific voice warning us in prophetic terms. There is no doubt in religious, political, or military circles that this physical world as it now stands will come to an end. To be sure, God is in command of history and will ultimately override all human activity to bring about his will.

Many lament the decline in the growth of Christianity, but be assured that God is alive and that there will always be God's remnant of the redeemed. We need never be discouraged or doubt if God is going to win against universalism, modernism, or materialism—in fact, he has already won the battle. A few years ago when Dr. Warren Hultgren and I went to Europe and Russia, we saw a movie on board the plane entitled, *The Battle of the Bulge*—which was a reminder of our struggle with Germany. This brought to mind the invasion and ultimate conquest on V-E day. The story of God's redemptive purpose for man can be seen in comparison. When our men stormed the beaches of Normandy and broke the back of the enemy, it was the turning point in the war for our forces. This event was called D day but the final complete victory didn't come until the armistice was signed and the enemy laid down their arms in defeat. When Christ died for our sins, he overcame Satan and assured his defeat for all ages. this was our spiritual D day but our V-day will only come at our Lord's return.

Religion of Future Shock

One of the most provocative books in recent years has been *Future Shock* by Alvin Toffler. This book has been read by millions and is required reading for thousands of high school and college students.

What are people referring to as future shock? How does this "Future Shock" affect us? The essence of it is that technological involvements are coming at such an accelerated rate that they will overwhelm the ordinary man unless he learns to cope with them. How to do so involves the spiritual life of a person, which puts man in the religious domain. The only way we can adjust and overcome the tension which develops is through the unchanging Christ, the same yesterday, today and forever.

The technological changes causing tension are many:

1. Travel is an example. The flight of a jet from nation to nation causes problems by the difficulty of a person adjusting to the fast change. Athletes who travel distances are usually not allowed to participate immediately or artists don't perform until there is a physical and emotional adjustment. Space travelers adapt to this by using space suits which the ordinary traveler doesn't have.

2. Science contributes to the problem. More than 90 percent of scientists who have ever lived are now alive. New products are invented and flood the market at such a rate that we must constantly adjust to change brought on by the pace of new products.

3. Physical environmental changes produce shock. We live in a throw-away economy. We throw away diapers, bibs, paper napkins, use nonreturnable bottles, even throw away wedding gowns and marriages. A lack of permanence is developed in the rental business such as Hertz cars, Avis rentals, clothes, and jewelry. A million things we use are no longer purchased and kept but rented and disposed of immediately. Even our apartment living suggests our unwillingness to make a permanent commitment to a location or house. The average

American family moves so frequently we have coined the term, "Corporation Gypsies," executives in the firm, who, to climb the promotional ladder must move frequently. This keeps our relationship with people very limited and changing.

4. Novelty reigns in all areas of life which reflect this disposition in fad clothes which change fashions overnight. The demand for situational toys keeps the public confronted with continuous change. The job pool reflects constant change in that one-half the jobs that will be available by 1985 have not yet been invented.

What is the by-product of "Future Shock" in our lives? It produces a tension resulting in emptiness, loneliness, boredom and despair. The despair of life, which means no hope, is reflected in all areas of our lives. It is seen in art, music, literature and philosophy . . . no hope, only despair. All expressions of our artistic ability reflect this spirit of hopelessness. It is this frustration which accounts for much of the psychosomatic illness of our times.

How will we adjust to this future shock and survive? We must remember "the earth is the Lord's and the fullness thereof." Realize that God is in charge of history, and he is moving it to an end which fulfills his purpose.

To maintain our sanity, to be meaningfully happy in this plight of future shock, modern man must have a God who is eternal, an authority that is relevant, and a fellowship that is meaningful.

A God Who is Eternal and Personal (Jesus Christ)

The God of the Old Testament was eternal because he was in the beginning. He expressed his relationship to man in the direct encounter of experiences. In the New Testament, God wanted to be more personal so he came in the form of a man. He wanted us to know him personally and to believe that he really cared. Jesus was God becoming more than eternal. He was personal.

God had an eternal purpose for man from the beginning of his creation. Sin entered into man's experience, but the love of God continued in his pursuit of fallen mankind. Throughout history God has manifested his plan of redemption in Jesus Christ. All of the Old Testament is God prefiguring the coming of his son Jesus Christ. The types and symbols of our Lord's ultimate personal appearance appear throughout all Scripture. One day God fulfilled the prophecy through Jesus from glory, stepping upon a cloud, then a mountain and into a stable. He came through the womb of a woman and lived among us as he walked the streets of our towns. He was the eternal God who became personal in Jesus Christ.

Who was and is Jesus Christ? He was and is God! We are told by Jesus, "If you have seen me, you have seen the Father." "My Father and I are one!" Jesus tells us in John, "In the beginning was the Word and the Word was with God, and the Word was God!" Jesus was God as is seen in his claims, his perfect life, and his presence before God now.

We could never have known who Jesus was unless he who was eternal became personal in his God-man relationship with us. The Bible says that he was the Word. Now I am using words and forming sentences and paragraphs to paint pictures in your mind. Words describe and illustrate meaning to the human mind. Jesus was the Word, God spelled out in syllables of love, joy, peace, and longsuffering. We never would have known God personally if Jesus had not spelled him out for us in words we could understand.

Jesus was man. He became man so he could understand our temptations and struggles. In all points he was tempted as we are, but without sin. There were names, attributes, and characteristics given to Jesus which only human beings have, so it proves his humanity.

Why did Jesus come? We know that Jesus came into the world, that he was born in Bethlehem, died on a cross, and rose again. People know that he came, but they do not understand *why* he came. He came to redeem us, pay the price which God's holiness demanded to bring us back to the Father. He did this by his substitutionary death on the cross for us. The cross was the place for sinful man to meet God's judgment. His love for us made him willing to provide his Son in our place. His resurrection then was God's attestation that he accepted what Jesus did in his death for our sins.

How does Jesus' death relate to you? By faith you can accept and appropriate the work of Jesus Christ on the cross for the needs of your sinfulness. An illustration can extend our comprehension of this great truth. Many years ago Thomas Edison invented the electric light and we benefit from it everyday. How is this possible when he performed his electrical miracle so many years ago? It is not necessary for him to invent again that I might have electricity. I only appropriate what he did years ago and it works for me today. The same principle is true today. Jesus does not need to die for us everyday; we appropriate by faith what he did nearly two thousand years ago, and it works in our lives.

Where is Jesus now? He is at the right hand of God the Father interceding for us. He is the divine mediator between God and man. The only way you can come to God is through his Son, Jesus Christ. God demands perfection to enter his heaven; and since man does not have perfection, we depend on the perfect righteousness of Jesus Christ.

Jesus who is now at the right hand of the Father will one day come again. He is coming back whether we believe it or not, whether or not we want him to, whether we are prepared or unprepared. Jesus is coming again to receive his church and to reject all who have rejected him. Every eye shall see him, and tongues confess him, and knees bow to declare he is King. Yes . . . the King is coming!

An Authority that is Relevant and Absolute

The existentialist says there are no absolutes, all things are relative; therefore, there is no code of ethics, no moral standards, and no spiritual guidelines to restrict and direct human behaviour. A thing is true or false, good or bad only as you think it to be.

There are absolutes, but they are not to be found in anything man has established but only in the established Word of God. It is absolute and unchanging in all ages. God has spoken, "Heaven and earth shall pass away, but my words shall not pass away" (Matt. 24:35).

The Bible is God's inspired Word. It is a compilation of sixty-six books written by men under the direction of God's Spirit. It was given to us by inspiration and can only be understood as God's Holy Spirit reveals truth to us. The purpose of God's Word is to be a guide for a troubled world, conviction for living, and a comfort for dying. This book is absolute when it speaks about:

Man—who was made in God's image but is unfulfilled until God fills his empty life with God's divine life. Man is in search of meaning and purpose for his life and will find it only in God. We are like God in our freedom, but our freedom misused brings results which separate us from God, our Creator, Savior, and Lord.

Sin—defined theologically, it is man's inordinate desire to have his will superior to God's. It is a rejection of God's plan for his life. Modern man's sin expresses itself in boredom, worry, fear, anxiety, and frustration. We are all sinners by conception, conduct, and condemnation. God's cure is the blood of Jesus Christ.

Death—the cessation of man's earthly existence. This does not mean that man ceases to exist. There was a time when we were not but then God created us in his divine image. There will never be a time when we do not exist, are not aware, are not conscious. Again, we are like God in that now we are eternal as living beings either with God or without God.

Judgment—that point in time when all men will stand before God and give an account of their lives. The Judge is one who can never be bribed, for his morality and character are perfect. All the facts of the case are evident because he knows all things and nothing is hidden from him. There are no favorites before his eyes for all men are created equal and judged accordingly. It is an inescapable appointment which God has made for every man.

Salvation—is God's free gift of eternal life to all who will receive him. It is not attained by works, ordinances, or man's righteousness, but is provided through God's grace and mercy for us. Grace is God's giving us what we do not deserve, and mercy is God's keeping from us what we do deserve.

A Fellowship that is Meaningful

Jesus said, "I will build my church; and the gates of hell shall not prevail against it." It is the only spiritual organism in the world built by our Lord. The only place you can find real spiritual fellowship is in the church. This is often referred to as the family of God, company of the committed, fellowship of the redeemed, and other references. All these terms suggest a spiritual home where believers have a sense of belonging and a challenge to grow. Jesus has assured us the church will never fail.

Where did the church come from? It was God's idea in the Old Testament to refer to his people, the Israelites, coming out of the wilderness as God dwelt with them in his glory. In the New Testament, he gave the "called out ones" the name of his church, and in Acts he finalized his plans by baptizing all believers into the body of Christ and making them his redeemed spiritual fellowship. Paul calls this the colony of heaven. God loves the church because it is that part of the world come home to God.

What is the church? It is a body of regenerate people who have been washed in the blood of the lamb and whose names have been written in the book of life.

What is the mission of the church? It is to do what Jesus did, that is, to reconcile men to God. He didn't always follow conventional methods: he performed miracles and raised the dead. Those activities brought condemnation from the religious leaders, but he did the work of God. Our task is to fulfill his purpose. We must do as a sign on a church read, "Anchored to the past, changing with the times." We remain committed to the basic fundamental truths and methods but are willing to innovate and adapt to make the gospel message attractive to people in need of Christ. We must speak to the times in which we live; and if we do not there will be no one present to hear when we speak.

Why do you need to be a part of a fellowship? First, to identify yourself with Jesus Christ. This is his church, his fellowship, his people; and if you love him, you want to be a part of him. Second, you need the encouragement and strength which comes from worship with God's people. Third, it is your place to serve him as a Christian. Jesus organized his church and gave it instructions to evangelize the world . . . you need to be a part of that effort. Fourth, to be obedient to your Lord for he commands we forsake not the assembly of ourselves together. The church needs you, and you need the church!

How can you become a part of a fellowship? You must hear the Word of God as it is taught or preached by someone. You must open your heart and mind to receive it as God's revelation to you. You then invite Jesus into your life as Savior and Lord forever. The moment you do the above you must next profess Jesus as did the Philippian jailer and be baptized.

Facing "Future Shock" need not overwhelm us if our lives are grounded in Jesus Christ.

We have a God who is eternal, on authority that is relevant and absolute, and a fellowship that is meaningful. These will brace our lives against every shock, present or future!

7

House to House Evangelism

"And have kept nothing from you but have taught you publicly from house to house." Acts 20:19

The biggest business in the world is winning lost souls to a saving knowledge of Jesus Christ as Savior and Lord. Henry Ward Beecher was speaking in the language of the Bible when he observed, "The greatest thing in the world that one person ever did for another is to lead him to Jesus Christ." God declares, "He that winneth souls is wise." Paul reminded the elders of his spiritual passion for the lost of their community, "I kept nothing from you but visited and taught you publicly from house to house."

Jesus designed and projected visitation evangelism. Visitation is scriptural. Evangelism is scriptural. Therefore, visitation evangelism is scriptural. Visitation evangelism is not only scriptural but difficult, in fact, it is the most difficult of all forms of Christian work.

Those who have tried to win men to Christ one by one know the task is not easy. It takes more real faith and courage to face a single sinner with the gospel message than it takes to confront a huge congregation. Personal evangelism is not easy, but why should it be? Work is not easy. Running a business is not easy. Ministering to the sick is not easy. In fact, all worthwhile human endeavors require the expenditure of energy and effort. Soul-winning, the greatest work of all, is no exception. It would be contrary to the laws of God in his world if leading individuals into a vital experience of redeeming grace were easy. As in all performances of tasks, winning people to Christ becomes less difficult with practice.

Personal evangelism is neglected. It is more neglected than any other form of Christian responsibility. People will respond to every type of call—from cleaning up the old church cemetery to raffling cakes for the new building—but pitifully few will answer the plea to win souls. The vast majority of the nominal disciples of Christ never open their lips to speak to other persons about their responsibility and relationship to God.

Thus, our greatest need in all of Christian endeavor is for a mighty sweeping revival of personal evangelism. History records that the armies of the Roman Empire were unable to win battles with long swords but when the military leaders invented the use of short swords which could bring soldiers into a closer personal contact with the enemy, they turned the tide to victory. Ours, likewise, must be a hand-to-hand combat with the world, the flesh, and the devil. For a Christian, church, or denomination to neglect this work of grace and not follow the pattern of Jesus is to commit spiritual suicide.

Personal evangelism is important. So important was it that Jesus preached and practiced it. He won every outstanding follower by the personal method. His early disciples relied heavily upon this plan for carrying forward the work of his kingdom. A close study of the beginnings of the Christian movement clearly reveals that it is God's will that every believer win others personally. It utilizes the church's greatest human asset, the individual member. Not everyone can preach, teach, sing, but *all* can witness. It is likewise important because of the dividends paid. It brings peace and joy to the individual and to the church.

Hear the Command of Christ

Jesus said, "As my Father hath sent me, even so send I you." Go. Every born-again believer lives under this injunction of Christ for the same blood of Calvary which converted our souls commissioned our service.

On one occasion as Prince of Wales, the late Edward VIII, was visiting the United States. He was entertained by a Washingtonian. The next Christmas the Prince, desiring to show his appreciation for the kindness extended him, sent his host a card. Since he did not know his host's winter address, the envelope carried on it the gentleman's name and USA. In the course of time, the card was returned to England with a note attached, "Cannot locate, insufficient address." The Prince sent the card back to America stamped with his royal signature and bearing on it the words, "Find this man." The card was delivered. So is it with the Great Commission—"Go ye" and find this man.

There are three good reasons for soul-winning which are similar to the reasons for fishing for fish. First, many people fish for food which provides the nourishment for physical life, but to fish for souls alone provides for the development of the spiritual life of every believer. Second, we fish for fun or delight. There is no more joy to be found in this life than that of helping a lost sinner accept Christ as personal Savior. Thirdly, many fish for funds, monetary value. All our work at present and in the future is dependent on our winning people to Christ. Unless this generation of Christians wins others, this may be the last period of Christianity! There will be no more church members, preachers, missionaries, denominational leaders, and every church will be closed for the duration unless we take Christ seriously.

There are other reasons why we must hear the command of Christ. The need of man! "Man has always been his most vexing problem," Reinhold Niebuhr says in *Nature and Destiny of Man*. The classical view, he points out, puts its emphasis upon man as a rational being whose unique distinction is his "mind" or "spirit." He continues, "Man is different from the animal kingdom in that he transcends himself, he can analyze himself and know himself." Nevertheless, man is a sinner by conception, conduct, and condemnation. A sinner by conception in that he is born with original sin and a sinner by conduct in that he lives in actual sin and a sinner by condemnation in that he has not believed.

The destiny of man without Christ causes us to hear this command. Man is not going to some intermediate state where we can make sacrifices or do penance for himself until he has enough merit to pay his way out of "purgatory" into Paradise. He is charged, sealed, and doomed to eternal hell "where the worm never dieth and the fire is not quenched."

A sense of Christian gratitude causes me to follow the example of Christ. Salvation is a gift and, therefore, a trust. It is not to be planted but revealed. Dr. Simpson discovered chloroform which could be used for the alleviation of pain and in a matter of hours the news was given to the entire world. We have the remedy for sinful men, but God is utterly dependent upon human intrumentality to reconcile this world to himself. In this chaotic hour, we must awaken to our sense of gratitude for what God has done for us and share it with every man to the end of the world. The forces of Communism, in its mad race to convert every individual to its philosophy of evil and destruction, must not be found more dedicated than Christians. Unless we awake, American freedom, businesses, homes, and schools are in for a spiritual eclipse. A revival of religion based on a world-wide personal soul-winning campaign is our only hope for survival!

Hindrances to His Command

Christ never issued a command which was impossible to perform. Nevertheless, there are many human hindrances before us which oppose evangelism.

There is, first, the caste system in our American way of life. We often speak of people who live on "opposite sides of the tracks;" therefore, we have classified people as easy, average, and difficult to win. Educational, social, and economic barriers keep us from winning some up-and-outs as well as down-and-outs. Our responsibility is to win every man regardless of color, clime, rank, file, or serial.

Lack of confidence in ourselves and a sense of unworthiness on our part serve as a hindrance. A sure cure for this is an assurance of your own experience, some knowledge of the Word of God, and a dependence upon the Holy Spirit for guidance.

Our greatest sin is not a lack of ability but a preoccupation with other things. We are so busy about things that are of secondary importance that we fail to major on majors.

Another problem is our feeling of intrusion into the right of another to do as he pleases about religion. If you were suddenly passing a house and discovered it on fire, I hope you would not hesitate to rush to the door and alarm the occupants of the impending danger. To save their lives from danger you would not think about personal feelings or have any hesitancy about the propitiousness of the occasion. You would quickly move in to do what you could about it. Men are lost without Christ, and this old world in which they live is on fire, so we must not hesitate to warn them of the judgment and of hell to come.

Perhaps the most insidious hindrance to winning people to Christ is our cold spiritual lives. The mere fact that we do not care enough to do anything about this most important matter is our main problem.

In our religious piety, we have become so cold-natured spiritually until our hot hearts of love have turned into cold-hearted pity for lost people. Nothing is more obnoxious to anyone than to have people merely pity them. A young woman came to her pastor to tell him that her husband had come in one night and told her he no longer loved her but merely had a feeling of pity. No more harsh, difficult, hard-hearted concern could ever come from the heart and lips of a companion. Change John 3:16 to read, "God so loved the world that he pitied it." This takes away the personal care, warmth, and compassion of God and leaves us more miserable in our plight. Our complacent pity must be set afire by a holy compassion of love for sinners who are in need of a savior.

Heed the Command

There are many factors which lead us to follow through in keeping this command of our Lord. First, we have the facilities with which to reach the lost. All across America we Southern Baptists have more than thirty-five thousand churches ranging from one-room country churches to the magnificent "cathedrals" in our crowded cities. Never have we had such modern, up-to-date equipment to use in reaching people and teaching the Word of God. Second, we have a tremendous faculty of Sunday School teachers, Church Training workers, Woman's Missionary Union members, Brotherhood workers, deacons, and all the other multitude of workers in our churches.

Third, we have a wonderful fellowship existing among us. No group of churches has as much to offer in a spiritual democracy as Baptists do. Here the American spirit of individuality and freedom prevails with every man before God with an open mind and an open Bible. Southern Baptist churches stand as a stalwart testimony to cooperation in carrying the gospel to all the world. In this type of warm fellowship, souls should come to life in Christ.

Any Christian can win people to Christ if he cares. First, he must have a divine assurance of his own salvation, know the Bible, and have faith in the miracle power of God to save, have a fulness of the Spirit of God to guide him in his endeavor, and pray for power in winning the victory.

Let us join in the immortal statement of Jesus in the garden of

Gethsemane, "Thy will be done." Nothing so charges us with strength to do as the decision of action. Resolve now, "I will do my best to win souls to Christ!" One difficult problem facing the average church is the feeling that the paid workers of the church will do the soul winning and that it is not the personal task of the other members. In early New Testament days, there were no differences in the laity and clergy—it was the personal responsibility of every Christian to share the gospel. When a chasm developed between the two, the laity and the clergy, we lost the personal concern for the lost and now must make every effort to recapture the concept of every man's task.

It is rather facetious for a church to announce, "This year we are going to major on soul-winning." It would be like the large paper mill in a city announcing in a full-page ad, "This year we are going to major on producing paper." There is no other task for the mill than to follow its purpose for construction. It has no other business! What business does any church have in existing if it doesn't seek to reach people to Christ? What right does a man have to stand in the pulpit and preach if he doesn't win souls to Christ? What right has a deacon, Sunday School teacher, choir member, or any other to serve if they are not soul-winners? The full obsession of every Christian should be to lead a soul to Christ.

Too many of our churches with multiple organizations are like the million-dollar post office built in Pittsburgh. The opening day was an incident of embarrassment because they discovered that in the expensive building everything had been provided with one exception. They had forgotten to place an open slot for the deposit of envelopes. The very purpose of the building was overlooked in the concern for the superstructure. The end of the means is often forgotten as we dally with the insignificant.

Our church organizational structure is designed for fulfilling the Great Commission. The Sunday School has as its basic function reaching, teaching, and winning people to Christ. If we return to this fundamental principle, we can win people to Christ. All organizations are challenged to use our WIN materials as tools to evangelize. Church Training is structured to teach all our people the *how* of personal evangelism. The only obstacle now is the preoccupation of believers in church programs which exclude the main task of the church.

Heavenly Results

Every one of us should long for the day when we can say: "God's will in my life has been done. I have won people to Christ." No greater joy will ever come to your life than the thrill of having helped someone make peace with God. All the other thrills of your life fade into oblivion in comparison to this wonderful, heavenly joy that floods your soul when you win a person to Christ.

Think of the joy it brings to the sinner who is saved. Never before has he been so happy since he first believed. He will wonder why he waited so long to be saved and will always be grateful to you.

Then there is joy in heaven when a person is saved. God's Word reminds us of the rejoicing in the presence of the angels and the redeemed. For example: a mother has prayed for a son many years; now she sees him saved and rejoices in heaven.

How are we to do it? First of all, we must talk to God about men—then talk to men about God. We can never do this great task without great prayer. Pray for yourself; pray for the sinner. Never stop praying. Then we must plead with the sinner about his need of a Savior. Never stop pleading. We must first begin at home, then go to neighbors and friends, business associates, and every person we can reach.

When we have all taken seriously the command of our Savior to win people from house to house, a miracle will occur. It is like the story Spurgeon tells of the mariner. He says:

Have you ever read the 'Ancient Mariner'? I dare say you thought it one of the strangest imaginations ever put together, especially that part where the old mariner represents the corpses of dead men rising up to man the ship. Dead men pulling the oars, dead men tugging at the ropes, dead men steering, dead men spreading the sails! I have thought what a strange idea! And yet I have seen that; I have gone into churches where there was a dead man in the pulpit, a dead man reading the notices, a dead man singing the solos, a dead man taking the collection, and the pews filled with dead men.

Suddenly these men have the spirit of new life fill them and they all man their position and the ship finds its cause to sail on. Personal and perennial evangelism in house to house soul winning will quicken any dead church and set it on fire to win a community to Christ. Set us afire, Lord.

Perennial Revival in a Church

Then they that gladly received his word were baptized: and the same day there were added unto them about three thousand souls. And they continued stedfastly in the apostles' doctrine and fellowship, and in breaking of bread, and in prayers. And fear came upon every soul: and many wonders and signs were done by the apostles. And all that believed were together, and had all things in common; and sold their possessions and goods, and parted them to all men, as every man had need. And they, continuing daily in one accord in the temple, and breaking bread from house to house, did eat their meat with gladness and singleness of heart, praising God, and having favor with all the people. And the Lord added to the church daily such as should be saved (Acts 2:41-47).

And the things that thou hast heard of me among many witnesses, the same commit thou to faithful men, who shall be able to teach others also (2 Tim. 2:2).

It would be absurd and facetious for me to give a plan of perennial soul-winning because the Master gave us the plan over two thousand years ago. Tragic indeed is the fact that the Communists have adopted this method from us and applied it to their organization. In a few years they have grown from 350 million to over 800 million subjects. They simply make friends with a person, win his confidence, and lead him into a state of mind where Communism becomes an obsession. He then in turn must select one with whom he will work, and on and on they multiply. So convinced are they that a young man in Korea was asked to prove his loyalty by kicking his mother's teeth out.

If this principle would be applied to our Christian forces and one of us would take a lost person and work with him for six months and lead him to Christ; then he in turn would take another and I would do likewise and in six months we would double again, and in six months again. We would win 4 in one year, 16 at the end

of two years, 865 at the end of five years, 1,769,472 at the end
of ten years. At the end of 15½ years, we could win the entire
world's population.

New Testament local churches were nerve centers of evangelism
and in this respect constitute a pattern for local churches of all
ages. Missionary evangelism had produced these local churches, and
they in turn made evangelism and missionary activity their main
business. We believe that this is the manner in which the divine
program should operate today.

Any evangelism which minimizes or overlooks the significance
of the local church falls short of true New Testament evangelism.
The New Testament knows nothing of evangelism apart from the
church. Without evangelism, local churches soon become corrupt
or die. Jesus said to Peter, "Upon this rock I will build my church
and the gates of hell shall not prevail against it" (Matt. 16:18). This
does not mean that the church is to be like a fortress holding out
against evil but, rather, that the church is to be an army on the
march storming the gates of hell, and hell will not be able to hold
out against its attacks. The picture is one of aggressive, perennial
evangelism.

The state of perennial revival is the normal condition of the church
of Jesus Christ. Just as a person's temperature can register below
normal, which indicates sickness, so the church can be below normal
in a lack of revival fervor and have a spiritual sickness unto death.
The men who oppose this idea set themselves against apostolic
religion and criticize the apostolic church, since the centuries have
seen few revivals such as that in which the church of Jesus Christ
originated. It is little wonder that the people have continued to
pray for a duplicate of Pentecost. Adding daily to the church, day
by day, those that are being saved, is the ideal, normal, healthy
state of the church.

As we discuss this problem, we must first adequately define terms.
What do we mean by revival? The dictionary says: "A renewal of
special interest in and attention to religious services and duties and
the subject of personal salvation; a religious awakening." Is that not
what the psalmist meant when he cried, "Wilt thou not revive us
again: that thy people may rejoice in thee?"

What do we mean by perennial? The meaning is: "continuing

through many years; unfailing, or unfailing perennial springs." The springs of revival have in too many churches been opened only at a certain season and remained in action for a very short time. Too many people near our churches are like the man in the Bethsaida porch. They have seen the waters troubled at a "certain season" and others stepping in to be made whole, while they must remain in their paralysis; for the waters grew quiet, and they knew that it would be a twelve-month period before the opportunity would return. Strange to say, many churches seem to forget that Jesus is at hand and can work the miracle of healing out of season.

The two words *revival* and *evangelism* are used interchangeably; however, for this discussion we refer to revival as that upsurge which takes place within the saints, and evangelism as that which transforms the sinner, or the winning of the lost to personal faith in Christ.

The pattern of perennial revival is found in plain and lucid illustration in the book of Acts. Here was a church with a constituency of 120, an organization with plans, a message from Christ, and a commission to the ends of the earth. Our churches today are similar in pattern and enduement. This church had great preaching, great personal work by the people, and a great program for world advance. Such is the plan for perennial evangelism.

The Pastor

1. Purpose to do it!

The pastor is the key to perennial evangelism in a church! He must know more, feel more, do more, and believe more about evangelism than any member of his congregation. The old adage is still true, "Like priest, like people." G. Campbell Morgan is right in saying, "Ours is not to catch the spirit of the day but to change it".

Andrew Blackwood says, "A pastor's failure is not due to his lack of ability or charm but to his lack of divine purpose." Far too many of us have many purposes in our ministry with evangelism being one of secondary importance. An Episcopal rector said: "I found myself engaged as the leader of the Community Chest, the Welfare Organization, the Rotary Club, and others until I had little time for my church. I suddenly realized that if I would drop out someone else would take the leadership and carry on as well; but if I let my church work go, nobody would do it." Someone else has said that if we would spend less time for humanitarian causes and win people to Christ, we could soon make these organizations useless.

Evangelism was born in the heart of the Savior and directed through the Great Commission and will not be fulfilled until every soul has heard the gospel. The big stick of the devil is to get the preachers to become so discouraged that they fail to believe that they can lead their churches in the never-ending task of winning the lost. Any man whom God has called to be a pastor can be a pastor-evangelist if he will have fresh experiences with God. What we need to do is to reexperience the suffering, death, and resurrection of our Lord!

2. Preach it!

For our example we turn to Paul, the fearless preacher. His message was adapted to the occasion but was always on fire for souls of men. Too much of our present day preaching is apologetic rather than authoritarian. People want to know, "What must I do to be saved?"

Spurgeon said, "I do not go far in my sermon until I cut straight across to Calvary." Dr. Perry Webb said, "We must be more than little preacherettes preaching little sermonettes to little Christian-ettes."

One leading Southern Baptist pastor declares that the modern preacher has turned from the conversion of the lost to the promotion of institutions and causes. We have proposed to save society in bulk: slum by slum, union by union, legislature by legislature, organization by organization. The young theologians have been preparing to redeem the world by becoming proficient in sociology. The average preacher in the modern pulpit is preaching themes that stress social ills rather than personal sin. Sermons have been centered in social and economic justice: the saving of democracy, the ills of the nation and world, pacifism, and the crusade for peace. If we are not discuss-ing world peace then we are occupied with race discrimination, international relationships, the promotion of cultural and fraternal movements, the necessity for civic improvements, the furthering of international justice. Having lost faith in the Scriptures and the power of God to save, we have found social subjects material for our sermons.

R. A. Torrey's statement is worthy of consideration: "I preach four great truths. I preach the whole Bible from cover to cover. I preach the power of the Blood of Jesus Christ to save . . . the doctrine of the Atonement. I preach the personality of the Holy Spirit. I preach the power of prayer."

A return to simple biblical evangelistic preaching is needed in every pulpit. Whether our method of preaching is the oratorical style of Frelinghuysen, the father of the Great Awakening, or the quiet, calm reader like Jonathan Edwards, we ought to preach a message from God to the hearts of the people. One preacher had it right when he said, "The business of the preacher is to take something hot out of his own heart and shove it into mine." The preacher's chief obstacle to evangelism is not his head but his heart.

3. Practice it!

Let the pastor keep before himself one perennial imperative! He must win men to Christ . . . or his ministry will go stale. He must win men to Christ . . . or his church will cease to grow. He must win men to Christ . . . or he will fail in fulfilling his ministry. Woe betide the pastor who becomes merely the administrator, the executive, the organizer, the good mixer, or hale fellow well met! The pastor should be concerned with compassion about every lost soul. It is claimed that when Tully was banished from Italy and Demosthenes from Athens, they were never able to look toward their homeland without bursting into sobs . . . such was their desire to be in their fatherland to help their people. To every pastor the thought of lost souls ought to be dearer than our homeland and to live without winning them more difficult to bear than banishment from the most comfortable environment of a luxurious, modern city.

There are many neglected fields—besides house to house visitation—where the warm-hearted pastor can win souls. First, a noble opportunity presents itself during marriages, where hearts are tender and sensitive and easily approached with counsel. Plead with them to make their home Christian and church-centered. In later years, the family will appreciate your guidance and your church will have life-long supporters.

Funerals—again there is a tenderness and sensitiveness of soul. Bring them comfort in the name of the Lord. Point them to Christ as the source of comfort. Dwell tactfully upon the uncertainties of life. Warn them to be ready for all the experiences that may come through loss, suffering, or death.

The People

1. Praying people.

The greatest sin of Christians is prayerlessness. Yet there can be no soul-winning fires to burn without the kindling of prayer on the part of the people.

The example of Jesus concerning prayer leads us to a conviction of our need. He prayed when he entered his public ministry. He prayed when he was baptized (Luke 3:21-22). He prayed for his disciples (Luke 6:12). He prayed for his evangelistic tour (Mark 1:35-38). He prayed before feeding the five thousand (Matt. 14:23). He prayed when he hung on the cross (Luke 23:34-36). He prayed in homes, highways, mountains, ships, and wherever he was.

No church can develop the lost art of winning souls apart from prayer. To develop this we can promote prayer-cards, prayer-partners, enlist shut-ins to pray, have extra prayer meetings, have special days of prayer and fasting, and lead the people into the habit of daily remaining in an attitude of prayer.

2. Working people.

There is no substitute for hard work. One of our leading Baptist historians recently listed the apparent reasons for the tremendous growth of Southern Baptists. He listed as follows: First, their adaptability to the situation. Second, we believe the Bible to be the inspired word of God. Third, we have stayed close to the people and have not developed a class-structured church. And lastly, we believe in hard work. No other type of evangelism demands so much of us in the way of time, energy, consecration, and downright disturbance of our precious schedules. It disturbs our pride, our routine, our complacency, and our ease. Redemption of lost men cost God too much for him to give it to our friends through us at cheap basement-bargain prices. It takes work! Churchill promised the people of England for their earthly security, "Blood, Toil, Sweat, and Tears." Christ promises us no less to find heavenly security for our friends and neighbors.

3. Spirit-filled People.

It must be remembered that each and all of the efforts must be under the immediate control and guidance of the Holy Spirit. We

may call this "experience," "sanctification," "second blessing," "renewed filling," or what not, but without it we are like a blind man
in a dark room chasing a black cat that isn't there. The Holy Spirit
will not lead us to bring every man to Christ but will empower
us to bring Christ to every man.

Our people must understand who the Holy Spirit is and why he
came into the world. We will not ignore this essential doctrine in
our preaching and teaching. We know that we are baptized by the
Spirit into the body of Christ—then he fills us as we surrender to
his control . . . this we call the filling. All churches need to be
filled with Holy Spirit-filled believers because they do not cause
problems, rather they solve them.

The Program

Great programs do not just happen. Great results are not accidental.
A hit and miss plan misses more than it hits. The only magic about
a perennial revival is perennial penitence, perennial prayer, perennial
preaching, perennial soul-winning, and perennial planning. I am not
much for organizing more units within the church; why not utilize
those we have already tried and found to be successful?

Begin with a church council on evangelism. Plan the church
calendar for the year and saturate it with plans for winning every
prospect to Christ. Every month have at least one special emphasis
to win the lost. See to it that every organization in your church
makes evangelism a priority. Delete finances, parties, trips, and
useless church meetings that don't have in them the ultimate purpose
of winning men to God through Jesus Christ.

The regular Sunday services provide our greatest opportunity. I
would not advocate a return to the pioneer spirit of barking, rolling
on the ground, and whinnying—neither would I advocate a dead
formalistic or liturgical service. More churches are interested in
keeping cool than in being on fire! In thousands of churches there
has been more warmth in the kitchens than in the sanctuary. Dining
rooms have buzzed with conversation and our prayer rooms have
been silent. Church programs have too often given over to "white-
washing" society instead of bringing individuals to a washing in the
fountain filled with blood. They have substituted reform for regener-

ation, new ideas for the new birth, a broad social consciousness for a deep God-consciousness.

For some unknown reason, we have fallen into the pattern of a message in the morning service for the saints and in the evening for the sinner, thus missing our many prospects.

These services ought to be permeated with an air of expectancy for results. Don't miss this opportunity of preaching to the lost, giving a warm-hearted personal appeal and having sinners coming to the altar.

The Sunday School is the best and most promising organization for the winning of the lost. It brings more lost into contact with the gospel than any other. The teachers are in small units with intimate contact to influence for Christ. Instill in the teacher's heart the responsibility of leading pupils to Christ.

Go before the Wednesday night teacher's meeting and constantly plead with them and ask for reports on soul-winning success. The pastor can set aside definite Sundays at which time he will go from department to department bringing brief evangelistic messages to the pupils. Train the workers to bring prospects to your study during the Sunday School hour and lead them to Christ. Study courses on soul-winning, winning the parents on Cradle Roll day, and other simple methods will result in the lost being saved. The Sunday School will either feed the church or bleed it.

Mission organizations literally mean soul-winning. The spirit of missions should make every member concerned for souls and active in witnessing. Too long have we complained that our mission organizations are interested in people beyond their reach whom they cannot become involved with directly. I refute this because in every church I have pastored, the most faithful witnesses have been our women involved in missions, Bible study, and evangelism. No church has need for a mission group who weeps for multitudes in other countries but will not cross the street to share God's love with the unsaved.

Today we are seeing a renewed emphasis on laymen becoming involved in the total ministry of the church, especially evangelism. Every church should encourage its laymen to be a participant in lay renewal and in our WIN program. Churches that have utilized these tools have seen a marvelous increase in baptisms and led our denomination in baptizing a record number of converts for three consecutive years.

Churches no longer must wait for special evangelistic campaigns to have revival. This ought to be happening in every church each and every Sunday. If we will give it priority and work at it during the week, God will give the increase when the people of God come together to worship on the Lord's Day.

Secret of Building a Great Church

Every believer, I trust, wants to be a part of what God is doing in building his church. God wants his church to be successful in today's world. The Bible reveals the basic principles required to build a successful, growing, reaching, New Testament church in any community. There is a responsibility for the preacher, people, and God.

The Israelites represent the children of God or the people of God. They, like the church today, were strangers in a foreign land in Egyptian bondage. They were the underground forces simply waiting for a deliverer. In due time God raised up his man, Moses, to lead them into the promised land. After all preparations had been made, the time of departure was at hand. In a military fashion, God's children marched out of bondage toward their prepared home. Satan is never pleased to let the redeemed go, so he hounded the Israelities by consequent compromises and ultimate attempts to defeat them.

After some time, the Israelites discovered they had come to an impasse. Ahead of them was the Red Sea, to the left were the Philistines, and to the right was the vast wilderness. A backward glance reminded them of the onrush of the vicious Egyptians. Here is one of the most lucid examples of how a group of people can be turned into a mob and stampede. Suddenly they became hysterical with screams of horror, caught like rats on a sinking ship, afraid every person would be killed by Pharaoh.

How like the Israelites are our great denomination and churches. Our history, from a small sect of despised people to a vast structure of almost thirteen million, reads like a romance and miracle. The only way we can rationalize our deliverance and accomplishments is in the light of the power and providence of God.

Through the years we have militantly marched from victory unto victory—but alas, we too have come to an impasse. We suddenly realize that our forward march is not as rapid and numerically successful as at other times. We are all bordering on hysteria, fears, and despondence. Many of our churches see before them the undisturbed waters of the baptistry. To our right is the uncertain wilderness of theological dispute and criticism. To our left are the ungodly Philistines of jealousy, criticism, and envy. To our rear are the vicious modernist, materialist, Communist, and others.

What can we do? Give up . . . no! When the Israelites faced this position they started to doubt God, criticize Moses, and dispute with each other, which only compounded their problems. There is no point in any phase of our work suggesting that our failure is due to the weakness of another agency—or that too much emphasis is given to one group when it ought to be given to another. In the midst of their confusion, God spoke to Moses and said, "Speak unto the children of Israel that they go forward." In the vernacular of the street . . . shut up and let God work!

The Preacher's Part . . . Speak

When God begins to make a way out of no way, the preacher has the first responsibility . . . that is to speak. The reason for his speaking is obvious. He is first to speak to enlighten his people in God's word. He must know many things in this complex church age; psychology, counseling, finances, promotion, and other fields; but let us always remember his first duty is to know the Word of God.

He is also to enlist his people in God's work. There are three classes of people in every church; the unenlisted and unsurrendered, the enlisted but not surrendered, and the enlisted and surrendered. The task of the preacher is to reconcile these groups into a New Testament fellowship, thus leading the whole church to proclaim the whole gospel to the whole world. It will demand the patience of Job, the wisdom of Solomon, the love of Paul, and the power of Jesus. Have you laymen ever tried to get all the members of your church in worship services? Have you ever tried to enlist them in Wednesday night prayer meeting, in Sunday School and Training Union, and then to tithe?

His next task is to evangelize the people in God's world. He is to keep before his people the fact that the world is our field. A church that does not give liberally to missions has denied her mission, and a church that does not reach out to win the community will dry up within her community.

The People's Part . . . Go Forward

The word "walk" is used throughout the Bible to denote how we are to live before God. In the New Testament, the concept is clear as we are commanded to walk even as he walked. Then how are we to walk?

First, we are to walk in love with Jesus Christ for his sake. In society, there is the pressure of desire to belong. We give loyalty and allegiance to unit organization in the church, but many people do not know what it is to love Jesus Christ. When we love him, it is evident in that we love his word, his work, and his people. Then our vocation becomes a vacation, our job a joy, and home a heaven. If there is a religious emptiness or a dissatisfaction, it is due to our lack of love for Christ.

We are to love each other for the church's sake. Jesus reminded his disciples, "By this shall all men know that ye are my disciples, if ye have love one to another" (John 13:35). God is love. If the church is the embodiment of God in Christ, then the church is love. If the church fails to demonstrate the love of God, it is a tragic failure; if it does so demonstrate it, it is a majestic triumph. The fruit of the spirit is love . . . just one, singular. The flavors of the fruit are many: love, joy, and peace. The love of the Christian is based on relationship to Jesus Christ. We love because he first loved us . . . not mere feelings, appearance, or agreement.

The love of the early church was built on the theological concept of the oneness of the body of Christ; and the whole body of Christ, which is the church, functions as a single body. That leaves no room for jealousy. You cannot conceive, in your own body, that one hand would tear another; that your fingers would pluck out your eyes; your teeth would purposely mutilate your own lips, nor voluntarily bite your own cheek. When a man is found cutting himself, you know that he is mad.

When someone sings better than you do, that is part of the body of Christ . . . your body . . . singing for you. When someone preaches better than you, he is preaching for you . . . your body is declaring itself.

The people of God can only obey the command of God in going forward if they walk in love with each other. We are to walk in love with souls for the world's sake. Our concern for the lost, world-wide, is our motivation of missions and evangelism. The two words, missions and evangelism, are often used interchangeably, but for our thinking we refer to missions as any and every effort used to reconcile men to God through Jesus Christ. Missions is that effort of making men aware of the presence of God.

A little boy stood looking at a picture of his father, killed in war, and said, "Daddy, come down from that frame." The business of missions is to take God out of history and make him relevant for today. This was the purpose of God in sending Christ from heaven, to a cloud, to a mountaintop, into a stable and through the womb of a woman to enter our human situation. The primary task of the church is missions. For that purpose it was born, with that passion it grew, and with that power it will cover the earth. The church was commissioned to work, to witness, and to win. The church is to preach a gospel of wholeness to the whole world. It must or civilization is sunk!

Evangelism is that fire in missions which makes it effective in carrying out the message of redemptive love. Evangelism is the heart of missions pumping vital life into every organization and effort.

Walking in love for lost souls will remind us of our mission of the Great Commission. A boy stood on the cold streets of a city looking into the frosted window of a cafeteria. A man passing by stopped to inquire of his problem only to be told that his parents had died and left him with no relatives. "Then who will feed and clothe you?" inquired the man. "Well, I am not worried," replied the lad. "My parents said they would tell God about me and He would tell someone to care for me." "Well," said the stranger, "if God told someone to provide for you, how is it that you are out here in the weather, cold and hungry?" "Well, Mister," said the shivering boy, "I know He told someone, but I guess they just forgot."

God's Part

In all the history of the Israelites, God met every difficulty and overcame it. He opened the waters of the Red Sea, guided them by night with a pillar of fire and by day with a cloud. When hungry, he fed them with manna and gave water from the rock. He provided them with clothes and shoes that never wore out.

As long as Israel walked with God, no nation could stand against her. She was not a military people, trained in the arts of aggressive warfare. Israel was no more than a group of farmers and shepherds who knew nothing but to depend on God. Seven heathen nations confronted them in the promised land, but God gave them victory over them.

There is no question in my mind but that God will solve every problem and provide for every need at home and abroad, if only we will meet God's conditions!

God has provided his power in the Holy Spirit. How long will it take us to realize that our accomplishments are "not by might or by power, but by my spirit, saith the Lord." We today are exactly like the church on the eve of Pentecost; we have an organization, a constituency, a command, and a Christ; but no power! There must be a revival of dependence on God. A. C. Dixon said:

> When we depend on organization we
> get what organization can do.
> When we depend on preaching we
> get what preaching can do.
> When we depend on singing we
> get what singing can do.
> When we depend on prayer we
> get what God can do.

Then the church must do the thing we least like to do . . . repent. Christ's last message to his Church was not the Great Commission. Jesus appeared in Revelation and commanded, "Repent . . . Repent."

Then we must recommit our lives, program, churches, and denomination to the task of carrying the gospel to the entire world. The story is told of a Scottish preacher, John Robertson. Once in a Scottish village the fires died in all the hearths and the people in the homes were freezing. A committee was organized to scan the community with hopes of finding some coal of fire to be shared with others. Desperately they sought from house to house but to no avail. At the point of utter frustration they decided to climb the hill and ask at one more home. To their utter delight they found a family hovering over a fire in their hearth. After an explanation of the problem the family agreed to share some of their live coals. Down the hill went the committee; first in this home to light a fire, then to another and another, until a fire was warmly burning on every hearth in the city.

Let's climb the hill called Calvary, get a new, live experience that will set our souls afire, then go back down into the valley to our churches and start a fire burning in everyone until the whole world can be touched by its warmth.

> Set us afire Lord, stir us we pray
> While the world perishes, we go our way
> Purposely, passionateless, day after day
> Set us afire Lord, stir us we pray.
>
> AUTHOR UNKNOWN

10

Let's Take to the Streets

We do not need to develop new methods of reaching people with the gospel; Jesus gave us his plan when he was with us. Going into the streets where men live and confronting them with the claims of Christ was the New Testament plan, and it has never been improved.

Our sophisticated generation is repelled by the idea of getting outside and beyond our cushioned pews and stained-glass windows, and this is the reason for stagnant church life. Every injunction of our Lord seems to ring with the divine command to take to the streets with the good news and share it with the masses. All who hear will not receive the invitation, but there are always some who will.

Every movement in history—to become significant—has had to take to the streets. I want to name several, without regard to our personal feelings relative to these movements, as examples of our challenge.

The rise of nationalism which has covered our world—with every small, struggling nation seeking freedom and independence—would have been impossible without these people taking to the streets with their cause. We recall that the labor movement was unnoticed until the laborers moved to the streets with their demands. The Civil Rights movement would not have made an impression on our society had it not gone to the streets with marches and demonstrations. College youth in revolt have challenged the status quo, curriculum, and educational supervision, and brought about some changes. Their threat to the old structure would never have been felt had they not taken to the streets with passion and purpose.

Business has become aware that to reach the masses with its product it had to move out of the corner store. Direct mailing to millions has made unknown companies household words. Moving out to shopping malls to stand at the crossroads of moving humanity has made taking to the streets successful. If we have failed to reach people for Christ, it is because we are disobedient to our Lord's instruction to "go into the highways and invite them to the wedding."

Early Church History

The early success of the Christian movement was due to the personal manner in which Christ was shared with people. There were no church buildings as we now worship in, so by necessity it had to be face-to-face confrontation. Socrates, one of the early philosophers, made this approach in his teachings. He was a "peripatetic," one who teaches while moving around. Jesus used this idea in his ministry and gave us the pattern whereby we were to relate the gospel to mankind. We can be peripatetics as we walk in and through the streets of our city sharing Christ.

The book of Acts is considered the history of the early New Testament church. The book of Acts records fifteen sermons which were preached by the apostles. These sermons were delivered in four different places: in the Temple (church), homes, jails, and in the streets. Only two of these sermons were preached in the "church," all others outside. Recall Paul's sermons to the Athenians and remember Paul's "pulpit" was out in the open. To make Christ's invitation effective, we must once again become bold in our willingness to go out into the streets with the message of redemption.

History Repeats Itself

Too many people consider the church a private religious club where they attend, sing, read the Bible, pay their dues, enjoy a message, and hope they won't be too disturbed by what is happening outside. Maybe this accounts for our hesitancy to take to the streets.

There are many changes which have occurred during the past few years, some of which have helped us recapture the spirit of the New Testament. As in every good cause, many have been carried to extremes, but some basic good has been derived.

The so-called Jesus movement has awakened within our culture a new desire to be bold in confessing Jesus Christ. Many youth of our country have tried to recapture the spirit and teachings of New Testament Christianity by abandoning our inordinate emphasis on material values. They have given up home, family, and security to become involved with a movement of love for humanity and Jesus. The staid church came to realize an element of truth in their proclamations and is now more open to a vibrant religious faith that expresses itself boldly.

The charismatic movement has brought us to a renewed study of the person and work of the Holy Spirit. Now there is in-depth study of this marvelous biblical doctrine. It has led many church people to become genuine Christians and many who were believers to understand how God came to live in them at conversion. It promises to give them joy and power for daily living. A new breath of God's heavenly presence is being experienced in many cold, dead congregations around the world.

Government officials are aware that they have tried to build on human ingenuity rather than the foundations of God as we know him in Jesus Christ. With the crumbling of governmental and political structures, men have turned to prayer breakfasts and retreats around the nation. There is a new dependence on God as religion has been carried to the streets.

For a while mass evangelism faded from our cities because of criticism which came from religious leaders. In recent years the cities, filled with violence, crime, and crusades of evil, have joined hands in united efforts to take the gospel to the stadium arena, and to the streets. Now mass evangelism is again in vogue, and the gospel is being preached to the masses.

Cold, dead, and formal music often has given way to the warm-hearted presentations of musicals which give testimony of our experience in Jesus Christ. The movement had its beginning in the youth culture and at first was repulsed by the older segment of our church membership, but now it is accepted by most. The musicals have taken to the open air, parks, auditoriums, and the streets of our cities.

Seminary enrollment is now at a record high in Southern Baptist institutions. God has been at work in all the new means of evangelism to save and call out young people who have answered God's call to the ministry. The openness of our churches to creative innovation has made it possible for God to work as he has been doing. The greatest mistake the church could have made was to resist the work of the Holy Spirit in taking the gospel to the streets.

Many local churches, once committed to the four walls of the sanctuary, have been willing to leave behind the stained-glass windows and cushioned pews for the stadium, city auditorium, and open-air revivals where the gospel was designed to reach the masses of unsaved people. The gospel will only live as it is declared in the open air and the streets, in addition to our church buildings.

Why Take to the Streets?

As we talk about taking to the streets, we actually mean taking the gospel to the masses wherever they are living. This is implemented by being aware that the cities are the population centers of our world, and it is here that we must concentrate.

Before the turn of the century, three-fifths of all Americans will be living in one of five giant strip-cities; the North Atlantic seaboard, the southern Great Lakes, the Florida, Texas, and California megalopolises. The urbanization of man is a new direction for population. It has produced a society with advantages and many disadvantages. The gospel, in method and application, cannot remain static in the face of this vast new challenge.

We cannot fail as a people of God to pray for divine guidance in capturing these cities for Christ. We are interested in the political and economic plight within these cities, but we must be aware that our main task is to evangelize. The church must reach out within the city where it is located to render social service to every need of people, but it must never be a substitute for our redemptive responsibility.

To begin fulfilling our tasks to cities, we must begin where Jesus did: he wept over the city. A spiritual concern bathed in the tears of a burden becomes our first tool in making Christ known to the masses on the street. The normal church in today's world is too smug and satisfied with the status quo. We will never win the world to Christ with our present spirit of apathy. As G. Campbell Morgan said, "Ours is not to catch the spirit of the day but to change it."

Today we must be willing to move through any door of opportunity to witness of our hope in Jesus. The crowded cities with its many streets filled with marching people without hope, is very impersonal. Existential loneliness prevails on every hand as people with a meaningless life move in circles that lead to nowhere. To meet their need, the gospel must be communicated to them in a dimension that is personal. The mass meetings, church worship services, and such are excellent ways to speak in generalities, but if man is to find identity and purpose, he must be personally confronted with the claims of Christ on his life. This can only be accomplished as every believer becomes committed to personal evangelism, sharing Christ in life-style evangelism. There are not enough evangelists or pastors to reach out and touch hurting people in our streets. It is every Christian's task to witness to every person in need. A new emphasis is being revived: the mutual responsibility of priest and people. All are to receive the Great Commission to witness to the ends of the earth. This is a laymen's movement which includes every sex, age, and nationality. Joining hands and hearts, we must move like a mighty army into the highways and hedges as Jesus commanded. We are God's salvation army and redemption center.

Every major denomination in our world has developed methods and materials to assist the total church membership in sharing Christ. This is the most encouraging sign on the Christian scene today. This is manifesting itself in little groups meeting to pray and study the Bible. It is a repetition of the New Testament "house church" which became so effective in spreading the gospel. It is interesting to note that in every part of the world where Christianity is growing at a rapid pace for the first time or where it is experiencing great revival, there has been a revival of the "house church." This is not to speak disparagingly of the church institutional, but rather to say we need both. The church as a location in a major facility is the training station to equip the saints to take to the streets with the good news.

Witness in the streets is restating the mission of the church. Jesus organized his church and said, "Upon this rock I will build my church; and the gates of hell shall not prevail against it." When he had finished, he gave to it the mission in this world. We might be in disagreement about the church's origin and organization, its ecclesiology and eschatology, but all Christian groups agree on its supreme mission.

The mission is best seen and understood against the background of a contract. We know that the mission is not political. It is not to say that the church ought not to be vitally concerned about the government in which we live. Surely we have a responsibility to speak out on every issue that affects the lives of people whom we seek to win. My only concern is that we realize this to be a secondary issue and not the main task.

It is not a social responsibility to feed and clothe humanity, thus, making a better way of life. The gospel does have social concern and relates to human problems, but never let the church get absorbed in humanitarian work and neglect the idea of salvation for the souls of men.

It is not educational progression. I believe in education, and we cannot do too much to educate our people and especially our leaders. However, we must recognize that education is not the end but only the means to the end of redemption.

Sheep feeding is important so some would have us believe that the task of the church is to run a sheep pasture, to educate, to worship, to elevate the saints to near perfection. This has been too long neglected, but if we major on feeding sheep, we will soon discover there are no sheep to feed. Jesus did not say stop and teach but rather go and teach all nations. Too much sheep stealing is occurring among churches. Some pastors and churches rejoice more over having a member from a neighboring church move his membership than he would rejoice in a lost soul. Our energy must be directed toward the unsaved and not to swapping fish in an aquarium.

We summarize the mission of the church by repeating our task of taking to the streets. Jesus stated it by saying, "Go into all the world and preach the gospel." This commission is from the heart of Christ, through the heart of the church, to the hearts of the world. The primary task of the church then is evangelism! For that purpose it was born, with that passion it grew, and in that power it will cover the earth. The church was not created to pet our prejudices or pamper our peculiarities. It was commissioned to work, to witness, and to win. It cannot exist as an organization of selfish souls satisfied with their own security; it can only move forward as a band of compassionate hearts preaches the gospel of a bleeding heart to the victims of a heavy heart. There can be no rest for the people of God until we have gone down every street of the world, sharing Christ in the power of the Holy Spirit. Let us begin today!

11

Can the American Home Survive?

A famed sociologist from England recently stated that in another generation "the home as we know it will completely vanish." This is possible if Americans continue their life-style which completely disregards the divine instructions of God given in Ephesians 5:21 to 6:5.

Dr. John Drakeford in his book, *The Home, The Laboratory of Life*, quotes Plato's words to the effect that the life of the nation is "only the life of the family writ large." Then what we see happening in our society—riots, murders, rape, and every form of crime—is an enlarged photograph of the American home. The greatest enemy to our nation is not foreign powers but the decline of homelife. Dictators like Hitler have known this and tried to destroy nations by destroying the home.

J. Edgar Hoover said: "There is no synthetic replacement for a decent home life. Our high crime rate, particularly among juveniles, is directly traceable to a breakdown in moral fiber—the disintegration of home and family life. Religion and homelife are supplementary. Each strengthens the others. It is seldom that a solid and wholesome homelife can be found in the absence of religious inspiration."

The home was the first institution which God created and ordained and is the most important. The home was the first institution in the Old Testament and the church was the first institution in the New Testament. God likened the two, the home and the church.

In fact, when the Bible speaks of the church it uses family language, because the church is the family of God. It uses the term "Father" which is a home term. The phrase "family of God" is a home term. In the early church believers called each other "brother" and "sister," home words. Christians in the New Testament wept together, rejoiced together, had all things in common . . . this reflects the togetherness of the home.

In reality the church is but an extension of the home. The spiritual life of the family is carried over into the spiritual life of the church. If a person is a troublemaker in the home, he will be a troublemaker in the church. If a person is a kind, considerate Christian in the home, he will be such in the church. The spiritual life of the home is enlarged and reflected in the life of the church.

The American home has reached a place of crisis. The dictionary defines a crisis as a point in disease when it is not determined if one shall live or die. America today is at the point where a spiritual awakening can turn us back to the ways of the Lord, or we can continue in our death march of rebellion against God.

The educator, theologian, and sociologist all give their answer to the question of cause. Some of the basic reactions are as listed below.

First, the complex social order in which we live makes it impossible for us to relate ourselves to each other in a family situation. We have less work and more leisure than ever before which results in the various members of the family becoming more involved in interests and activities beyond the home. This absence from family unity and fellowship causes a breakdown of the family structure. There is no time to live, love, work, and worship together due to other involvements.

Second, the materialistic spirit of the day causes us constantly to strive for things and gadgets until we lose sight of the real values of life. In trying to "keep up with the Joneses," we fall out of step with God. There is no time for the family to play or pray together because both parents are working, when many times this is not necessary. There is a tendency for many men to have a basic job, then a second or even a third job, in an attempt to provide more things for their families. In reality they are often giving their families things, rather than themselves, which is a poor substitute.

Third, the new rise in the independence of women. This is not bad within itself because every individual is made in the image of God and has equal rights. In God's design for the human family, he made the opposite sexes and gave them a role to perform in replenishing the earth. This family would have respect and responsibility. This is a law of God woven into the Bible and society and like any other law of God, if disregarded, brings problems.

The tendency of role exchange in the parents is frustrating to the children. When the son comes home to find Mother wearing blue jeans, mowing the yard, and father with his apron, washing the dishes, he is unable to identify with his proper male sex. Some have advocated that this swap of roles, attire, and leadership in the family has created many of our homosexual problems. Let us get back to the basic plan of God.

Fourth, the individualism of the various members of the family. Everyone has his own interests, job, car, friends and money; thus, no feeling of dependence on the other members of the family. This attitude of selfishness overrides the responsibility we have to the family desires and needs, and causes a breakdown in the relationship. We must return to the biblical teaching on love, family, and marriage if we are to save our homes and ultimately America.

Woman's Relationship to the Husband

Paul writes the injunction in Ephesians 5:21 against a very unusual background. Before his time, women were not persons but merely things. With the coming of Christianity she was given dignity and equality. To give women protection and rights in the family situation, Paul dealt with her role to husband and family members. No other individuals in history owe as much to Christ as women. In spite of her liberation, the modern woman is dissatisfied and perplexed.

A leading anthropologist has said that in spite of the fact that American woman has more than any woman in society, she is more dissatisfied and discontent because she does not know her role or refuses to play it. Her role is equality with but not superiority over her husband.

Sometimes women refuse to be obedient to this text on the grounds that their husband is not capable of being the head of the household. Like a woman who said to her husband, "You are not the man I married ten years ago," to which he replied, "I guess not . . . you have changed me seven times."

Again they will say, "My husband is not a Christian and the Bible reminds us that we are not to be unequally yoked." Though this be true, the New Testament reminds us that if a Christian is married to an unbeliever, he is to remain with that unbeliever and win him to faith in Christ.

Therefore, husband and wife have basic emotional, spiritual, and physical needs and they must not keep themselves from each other except by consent. There is no room for selfishness or frigidity in the Christian home.

Though a woman is to be "subject" to her husband, she is not to be a slave to him. Matthew Henry wrote in 1763 the following, "When God made woman, he did not take her from his foot to be trampled upon, from his head to be lorded over, but from beneath his arm to be protected, and near his heart to be loved."

Relationship of Husband to Wife

Even though God reminds us the wife is to be subject to the husband, He protects the woman by giving the man a directive to love his wife as Christ loved the church (Eph. 5:25). How then did Jesus love his church?

It was a sacrificial love. Jesus loved the church and gave his life for her. He never thought in terms of what the church could do for him but rather what he could do for the church. He served, loved, and protected the church as the husband is to be related to his wife. When this characteristic reigns, there will be no abuse, rudeness, impoliteness, or neglect.

It was a purifying love. Jesus purified the church by "the washing of the Word." Any love which is real gives dignity to the marriage partner and does not drag him down to a second-class role. It does not seek mere physical gratification without consideration or pure love being involved. Often by "love you" mates mean simply a thing to be used or misused rather than a self-giving. This attitude is base, carnal, and lustful.

It was a caring love. As a man loves and cares for his body, even so ought he to nourish and care for his wife. He is to provide and protect her in a home situation where she can grow intellectually, physically, and spiritually.

It was an unbreakable love. As man leaves his father and mother, he is joined to his wife forever. Since physical union made man and woman one in Christ, only cohabitation outside marriage can dissolve this union and make the innocent part free from the unbreakable bond of marriage. This is why Jesus states concerning divorce, "save for fornication."

Children's Relationship to Parents

The children have a responsibility to their parents—obedience (Eph. 6:1). As long as a young person lives in the house provided by his parents, eats their food, wears their clothes, spends their money . . . he or she is to be obedient to them. Now, you may not enjoy being obedient but you must. When a young person gets to the place he is not willing to obey his parents, he ought to pack his belongings, get out of the house, make his own living, and be his own boss. As long as he refuses to do this, he is bound by the Lord to obey.

God protects children from parents who would take advantage of their authority by reminding them not to provoke children to anger, but "bring them up in the nurture and admonition of the Lord."

Parents have a right to expect obedience, respect, and love from their children and children have a right to expect some things from parents.

First, a godly Christian example: Youth are rebellious to shallow hypocrisy. One college professor said recently, "The youth rebellion is the expression of a dissatisfaction over the values their parents have had in life." They have seen in us a desire for material over spiritual. The bank balance is the status symbol. Parents talk about honesty and their children know about their dishonesty. They tell children about spiritual values, go to church and give fifty cents—then go and buy a twenty-dollar meal. Soon, youth know their parents are saying one thing and practicing another.

Second, a Christian faith. We establish standards for our children in nearly every area of life and try to influence them in that direction. When it comes to religion or spiritual things we bow out by saying we don't want to interfere with their decision. We have a responsibility to create a Christian atmosphere, pray with them, explain the meaning and way of becoming a Christian, and urge a decision as they grow old enough. Joshua had the right role, "As for me and my house, we will serve the Lord." What about you?

12

For Preachers Only

Ministers need to be reassured that the message they preach is given of God. He prepared it, and we are to declare it. I do not propose to discuss with you the matter or method of sermon preparation; that is, what books to read, courses in seminary to take, and the like. My object is to tell you about a message that has already been prepared and given to us who are preachers. I do not refer you to Bultmann, Buber, Tillich, or other contemporary authorities, but to the one authority—God's Word.

Many things in the Bible are hard to understand. If Peter found Paul's writings hard to understand, as he stated in 2 Peter 3:16, "As also in all his epistles, speaking in them of these things; in which are some things hard to be understood," you may be sure that you and I find many things in God's Word difficult.

However, there are two things made plain, open, and evident. One is that God prepares his messengers for the task to which he has called them. Listen to Jeremiah 1:5, "Before I formed thee in the belly I knew thee; and before thou camest forth out of the womb I sanctified thee, and I ordained thee a prophet unto the nations."

Jeremiah was as sure of his call as he was of his name. It was his destiny under God to be a prophet. Hear Isaiah 6:7-9: "And he laid it upon my mouth, and saith, Lo, this hath touched thy lips; and thine iniquity is taken away, and thy sin purged. Also, I heard the voice of the Lord, saying, Whom shall I send, and who will go for us? Then said I, Here am I; send me. And he said Go, and tell this people." Isaiah knew God had called and prepared him.

Focus on Paul in Galatians 1:15-16, "But when it pleased God, who separated me from my mother's womb, and called me by his grace, to reveal his Son in me, that I might preach him among the heathen; immediately I conferred not with flesh and blood."

God called him by his grace and revealed Christ in him that he might preach. Brethren, we must be as dead sure of our call by God as the prophets and apostles of old.

Remember this—God never prepared a man to preach whether he be prophet, apostle, or New Testament preacher, that he didn't give to that man a prepared message. Jeremiah 1:7-9 says: "But the Lord said unto me, Say not, I am a child; for thou shalt go to all that I shall send thee, and whatsoever I command thee thou shalt speak. Be not afraid of their faces: for I am with thee to deliver thee, saith the Lord. Then the Lord put forth his hand, and touched my mouth. And the Lord said unto me, Behold, I have put my words in thy mouth." Isaiah 6:9 says: "And he said, Go, and tell this people, Hear ye indeed, but understand not; and see ye indeed, but perceive not." Paul affirmed in Galatians 1:11-12: "But I certify you, brethren, that the gospel which was preached of me is not after man. For I neither received it of man, neither was I taught it, but by the revelation of Jesus Christ." Paul reminds us that he received his message from God.

God calls a man, prepares the man, and then commits to this prepared man a prepared message. We do not guess the message, accidentally stumble upon it, or originate it. All we do is to proclaim it!

What is this message? Listen to Paul again in 1 Corinthians 15:3-4: "For I delivered unto you first of all that which I also received, how that Christ died for our sins according to the scriptures; And that he was buried, and that he rose again the third day according to the scriptures." God was in Christ, reconciling the world unto himself. God in Christ—Incarnation—reconciling the world—atonement. The message is that God had come in Christ to redeem the world. The gospel begins with a baby in a cradle and ends with a man on a cross who arose the third day.

This Is the Prepared Message

1. First of all, God thought it out in eternity. He saw man's sin and his need of redemption and thought out how it could be accomplished in the light of his own holiness and love. God saw the plight of sinful men and invaded the human situation in Jesus Christ. God's plan of redemption didn't begin at Calvary but with the need

of the first man. Francis Thompson's "The Hound of Heaven" adequately pictures God searching for man from the beginning of man's despair. This is ultimately the sovereignty of God or his initiative in providing a way of deliverance. Man's redemption was thought by God, bought by Christ, and wrought by the Holy Spirit.

2. He not only thought it out but revealed it in the types and sacrifices in the Old Testament. The Passover teaches the Christian that death comes to everyone who is not covered by the blood of Christ. The Day of Atonement teaches that without the shedding of blood there is no remission of sin. The sacrifice of the lamb on the altar teaches that the lamb of God would take away the sin of the world. The scapegoat, on whom fell the sins of all the people, teaches that one would come who would take our vile sin in his own body on the cross.

3. God not only revealed the message, but his prophets proclaimed it. As in contemporary experience, the Israelities didn't accept it and many rebelled against it; however, the prophets continued to thunder out the prepared message. Even though their main task was to be forth-tellers and fore-tellers, there is a gospel note of messianic hope running through all their messages. The prophet Isaiah proclaimed a new sacrifice not of animals but of a person. Jeremiah proclaimed a new covenant with Israel and Judah which demanded an inward experience. Ezekiel preached the need of a new nature and a new heart. Daniel foretold a new king and new kingdom that would demand no new sacrifice but direct knowledge of God. Joel proclaimed a new experience when God's Spirit would be poured out on all flesh. Habakkuk declared a new salvation that would come, not through faithfulness but through faith.

4. Jesus taught this message to his disciples; brethren, if you have ears to hear it, Jesus himself didn't originate this message. In John 7:16, he said, "My doctrine is not mine, but his that sent me." He himself received it. Did he not teach in the third chapter of John, that as Moses lifted up the serpent in the wilderness, even so must the Son of man be lifted up? Did he not teach in the fourth chapter of John that God would no longer be worshiped in one temple, but everywhere? Did not our Lord at his own Supper, take bread and say, "This is my body broken and blood shed for you"? All our Lord did was teach a prepared message.

5. This is all the early church preached. They simply preached what they had received. They met in catacombs and read the Scripture, gave testimony as to their experience with Christ, prayed, then went out to tell others of him. The message of the church was the gospel of God.

What Does this Gospel Accomplish When We Preach It?

The gospel! Paul loved that word and the sound of it. He spoke that word often. He confessed that the gospel of Christ was the power of God unto salvation to everyone that believed.

Yes, armed with that one word the early Christians conquered much paganism of the Roman Empire. With that one word, "gospel," Luther, Knox, Calvin destroyed the darkness of the Dark Ages, broke the back of the Roman Catholic Church, and ushered in the Reformation. With that one word, "gospel," John Wesley and John Whitfield held back the force and flow of infidelity and immorality that already flooded France and were seeking to swamp England.

With that one word, "gospel," Jonathan Edwards fanned the fire that led to the First Great Awakening in the United States.

What else made Charles Spurgeon different? With only the gospel, Spurgeon as a nineteen-year-old boy had the nobility of England sitting at his feet. Space forbids me to mention the conquests of men and women who armed themselves with one word, "gospel."

Of course, as ministers, we are to know higher criticism, science, philosophy, liberalism, neo-orthodoxy. But know this also, God has not put one gram of power to save an individual or bring him from darkness to light in any of these systems. The power is in the gospel that proclaims his Son. The gospel and the gospel alone is the power of God unto salvation.

The gospel has power to change a church. When the gospel is at the heart of a church, it becomes literally a "salvation army." The command of Jesus to his church was to go throughout all the world and preach the gospel. For that purpose it was born, with that passion it grew, and in that power it must cover the earth. The church was not created to pet our prejudices or pamper our peculiarities. It was commissioned to work, to witness, and to win. It cannot exist as an organization of selfish souls satisfied with their own security; it can only move forward as a band of compassionate hearts preaching the gospel of a bleeding heart to the victims of a heavy heart. The gospel will make the church realize that "evangelism is the fire department of the church and when it moves in everything else must move out."

The gospel will give the church a new power. On the day of Pentecost the Holy Spirit empowered the church so she could then go out and proclaim the gospel of the Son of God. We are like the church—on the eve of Pentecost—which had the organization, constituents, and commission of Jesus but no power. When a church will stay with the gospel, the Holy Spirit will breathe upon it and make its message and ministry effective.

The gospel will change a preacher! Too many of us have lost faith in the power of God to transform human lives. We have adopted the thesis of William Ward Sweet who stated in his *Revivalism In America*, "Revivals were born on the frontier and since the frontier has passed so has revivalism." What he failed to consider was that revival was born in the heart of God and will last until every lost sinner has accepted Jesus as Lord.

R. A. Torry has said that the gospel can still change people as long . . .

as hearts are still broken by sin.

as hearts cease to be satisfied by pleasures of this world.

as the Holy Spirit convicts men of sin, righteousness, and judgment.

as the gospel remains the power of God unto salvation.

as men in simplicity and faith have courage to declare it.

The gospel will make a preacher effective for God. After the death of Jesus Christ, there was the preaching of the Apostolic Fathers and then the Greek and Latin preachers. The latter marked a period of coldness in their presentation of the gospel. One writer accredits this to the fact that they had not experienced the life and death of Christ as the apostles. Then what we need to do in order to be effective for God is to reexperience the suffering, death, and resurrection of our Lord.

The gospel will give a preacher fire. People are not interested in the theories of the atonement, the exegesis of *Logos*, the subscripts of New Testament writings, or the moral involvements of Hammurabi's code. They want to know how the gospel can come into their lives and change them to meet the present problems of contemporary life.

How Are We to Preach this Prepared Message?

1. With full dependence on God. The branch has one responsibility: to stay in union with the tree; it is the tree's responsibility to provide sap, bud, blossom, and fruit. We are not responsible for success, crowds, conversions, churches to pastor. Our responsibility is to stay in union with Jesus Christ, then it's his responsibility to do everything else.

2. We are to preach this message with steadfastness. Paul said, "We are to preach the gospel in season and out of season." Brethren, it's easy to preach the gospel in season when there are no open problems in the church, when our salaries are good, crowds are excellent, finances wonderful, additions perennial. Anybody can preach in season, and nobody enjoys preaching in season more than I do.

The test of our love for Jesus Christ and our call to the ministry *is to be able to preach it out of season.* Out of season when God hides his face from us and we see no results and we despair of solving the problems in our churches. Tell me, was Paul always a success? What do the Scriptures say? He was lowered in a basket over a wall in Damascus, they ran him out of Thessalonica, sneered at him in Athens, they imprisoned him in Philippi, they tore off his clothes in Ephesus, and left him for dead in Lystra. But Paul got up with his wounds still open, his blood not yet caked on his back, his body mutilated, and half-naked, and he continued to preach the gospel. We can imagine Paul with his head on the block, his final departure at hand, the executioner standing over him with ax in hand; but as that ax came swishing through the air, Paul cried with a loud voice and said, "Friend, believe on the Lord Jesus Christ and thou shalt be saved." The next moment Paul was in the presence of his Lord with the gospel still on his lips. He preached the gospel in season, but he also preached it out of season. We must have this kind of steadfastness that we can say, "I have fought a good fight, I have finished the course."

3. But also, we must preach this message with *awesome* urgency.

Our task is urgent because of:

A call from God, "Woe is me if I preach not the gospel." Time and again the prophet said, "The burden of the Lord was upon me."

God's holy nature. "Knowing the terror of God we persuade men. Our God is a consuming fire. The wrath of God is revealed from Heaven against all unrighteousness and ungodliness."

The sinfulness of men. Worlds colliding, bombs exploding, civilization in upheaval and unrest. What causes all this? The heart of man is still desperately wicked and deceitful above all things. Man with his laws, higher wages, better working conditions, improved education systems, and time-saving gadgets is still sick in his heart.

Our church members are backslidden. Enough said!

The coming of the Lord Jesus. I don't care whether you are post-millennial, pre-millennial, or a-millennial—you do not stand in the line of the true succession of apostles and early Christians unless you preach the return of the Lord Jesus Christ. The Bible tells us that when our Lord returns he will come in flaming fire, taking vengeance on them that know not God and obey not the gospel, who shall be punished in everlasting destruction from the presence of the Lord.

Confident assurance. With assurance in our hearts that we are in God's hands and he cares for us. No matter where you are preaching the gospel, in catacombs or cathedrals, he is ever watching over you. Shakespeare said: "For thy sweet love remembered such wealth brings, that then I scorn to change my state with kings." Preachers, you are more important in bringing this world to God than presidents or kings. We are New Testament preachers of the gospel of the Son of God.

We are confident in the ultimate victory of his cause. Ours is not a battle which could possibly suffer defeat; ours is one where victory has already been assured. For example, D day was a decisive battle in World War II. From the beaches of Normandy, across France, and ultimately into Germany, our soldiers marched. D day was the day the war was won, but the fighting continued until V-E day when the war in Europe was ended. There is a parallel to this in Christian history. The battle was fought and won on Calvary, where sin and death were defeated forever. We can be sure the victory is ours! However, the battle continues day by day until the ultimate consummation in the coming of Christ. His death was our D day and our V day is in his coming again. The point at hand now is our willingness to share in this victory and help others to share in it until we sing: "Hallelujah! Hallelujah! The Lord God omnipotent reigneth forever, and ever, and ever!

13

A New Philosophy

We are living in such a world of business until it is not unusual for us to relate profit and loss to the experiences of life. This question, "What profit hath a man of all his labour which he taketh under the sun?" is pivotal. Man rises early in the morning, works all day, and retires late at night. He lives through many years, even seventy or eighty. When all of this is done and man's works, deeds, and aspirations are all summed up and totaled, then what profit is it all? In brief, "What is the use of it, anyhow?"

All of us could be placed in one of two schools of thought: The first is that man is born, will live in futility, and die within a few years, the average span of life being about sixty-eight for men and seventy-one for women. The other is that man is a soul created in the image of God. Man is on the earth for a purpose and that is to honor and glorify God. When he dies, he passes into his eternal abode prepared for him before the foundations of the world.

Man and life are two pertinent subjects today. Analysts are trying to dissect these two and understand them as one would the working of a mathematical problem. Some of the recent definitions of man's problems and dilemmas are as follows: Karl Marx says that the problem of life is economic. Too few people have amassed the wealth of civilization, thus depriving the multitudes. The solution to this is economic revolution, distribution of wealth equally among all men, thus making every man a king.

John Dewey refutes the above to declare man's problem is an educational one. We have made such tremendous strides scientifically that we have been unable to develop mentally so as to keep the two abreast. Thus, the solution is to educate man properly, giving him knowledge to work out his dilemma.

Sigmund Freud would advocate that man's problem is emotional. All impulses and drives of the personality are derived from the basic sex urge. Thus, many people have interpreted Freud to mean that the solution is to permit life to be a free expression of sex in any manner or form. This results in sex delinquents, sex perverts, trial marriages, and easy divorces.

God's view is that man is a sinner. He is a sinner by conception, under the guilt of original sin. He is a sinner by conduct, under the actual sin. He is a sinner by condemnation, under the guilt of God's judgment. Therefore, man's hope is in deliverance, salvation, redemption, conversion, a new nature in Christ Jesus.

There Are Two Factors in Life

The life of each one of us is divided into two factors . . . the means by which we live and the ends for which we live . . . and nothing enters much more deeply into determining the quality of a man or an era than the handling of these two factors. This is easily illustrated in terms of the generation as a whole. The fact distinguishing our day from previous times is obviously our mastery over the scientific means of life. One after another the forces of the universe, from steam to the impalpable division of the atom, have been harnessed for our service, until we possess, as no previous age even dreamed of possessing, the means of living.

A few years ago I stood in the ruins of Athens, Greece, and remembered the Periclean Age when around the Acropolis gathered a people who preserved for us a culture which has been an inexhaustible goal for our new world. To note the means with which they lived, they were in the backwoods but when we think of the ends for which they lived they were on boulevards.

To walk along the shores of blue Galilee is to remember the little group of disciples following Christ. The provisions for life were crude but their passion for life was catching. Seeing their lack of "things" would let us know they were subjects for federal relief, but the purposes they possessed made them princes, kings, and presidents. Contributions made by them were more effective for world peace than all of the United Nations' machinations of our modern era. They had no conveniences of life but convictions, no program but a purpose, no new deal but an ideal, no possessions but an obsession, no means in life but a mission for life.

We have been living in a day when our main dependence has

been on humanism and materialism, but the voice of Jesus speaks out and is right. Something else must be considered first—God—or else all the materialistic inventiveness of man will explode in our faces to destroy the homes, businesses, cities, and souls of men on a scale unbelievable.

Two Testimonies of Such—Solomon and Paul

The two views of life are clearly expressed in the attitude of these two characters that I want to introduce to you. First, there is Solomon. Without question he is the author of Ecclesiastes. He looks upon life through dark glasses. He is a pessimist, so to speak. God gave him the chief desire of his heart, wisdom; in turn he tried every avenue of pleasure to decide what is best for man, yet no peace came to his soul.

Here was a man who can find nothing good in life, people, or the future. He of all men must have been most miserable! Here is his analogy of the profit of life, "Vanity of vanities, all is vanity. What profit hath a man of his labours? One generation passeth away and another cometh, but the earth abideth forever. . . . The wind blows in all directions yet returns by its own circuits. All the rivers run into the sea; yet the sea is not full; from the place the rivers did come they return again. My eyes see but are not satisfied, my ears hear but are not filled. There is nothing new under the sun, no nothing. Can any man say, see this new thing?"

Here was a man who had access to every human advantage of life, yet in it all he did not find happiness, peace, or purpose. This is the spirit of a character in one of George McDonald's books who said, "I wish I had never been made." One writer said, "The only thing about life I would change would be to have never been born."

This type of person, if his bread would fall butter-side down, would declare that all the Jersey cows were dead; and if he were in the ocean with a leaking boat, he would declare it the fault of the ocean. Alexander Maclaren said, "This cynical cynic says everything looks yellow because his own biliary system is out of order." It is this attitude that possessed Martin Luther when his wife asked, "Martin, is God dead?" Life built on this philosophy is bleak and vapid.

We live in a day when mental institutions are bulging with patients and applicants. People are facing problems, nervous and disturbed;

thus, thousands are going to psychiatrists, consultants, and fortune tellers. The fact remains that many of them need only the peace of God in their souls to calm the sea of restlessness which comes by removing the guilt of unforgiven sins. God is the answer!

I introduce you to another Jew. This man had all reasons to be pessimistic, blue, despondent, but he was not. See him as a Jew among his people, a Pharisee, a member of the Sanhedrin court, a brilliant leader. He left all to follow Christ. He was ostracized! Hear him, "I was stoned, beaten, and left outside Lystra for dead. I was shipwrecked, starved, striped forty times save one, then finally locked in prison in Rome. This I counted joy for all things have happened for the furtherance of the gospel. Oh! brethren in Philippi be not dismayed for I would have you know, for me to live is Christ but to die is gain."

Reasons for These Two Views

Here are two men with the same nationality, characteristics, and background, yet they viewed life oppositely. Solomon thought it was his to catch the spirit of the day, but Paul thought it was his to change the spirit of the day. There was some reason for this difference in philosophy.

For a long while Solomon had his eyes fixed upon himself. His chief attributes were envy, jealousy, selfishness, pride, and egotism. Everything was "my" and "mine." He had no interest in anything apart from himself.

Paul's life was different; he had his eyes fixed on a point outside and apart from himself and that was Jesus Christ. Hear now his immortal vow, "I count all things loss that I might gain him." His attitude was such because of his experience with Christ in salvation. To Paul the Lord Jesus Christ was more than a convenient fire escape out of hell, and his blood more than a handy rinse.

Solomon was a conquered man. The fears and frustrations of life were more than he could withstand. Life to him was as one cynic replies, "I pity young men today. If I were such and lived, I would jump out the window and end it all." If you are committed to folly, failure, futility, and frustration turn to Jesus Christ alone who gives peace.

Paul was a conqueror—"I can do all things through Christ who strengthens me." He felt the divine presence of God with him in every experience of life, and you can have this assurance, too. One of the most moving scenes in English literature comes at the end of Dickens' *Tale of Two Cities*. The carts were rumbling through the thronged street of Paris to the guillotine. In one of them were two prisoners: a brave man who was giving his life for a friend, and beside him a girl, little more than a child. She had seen him in the prison and had observed the gentleness and courage of his face. "If I may ride with you," thinking of the last dread journey, "Will you let me hold your hand? I am not afraid but I am a little weak, and it will give me more courage." So they rode together, her hand in his; and even when they had reached the place of execution, there was no fear in her eyes. She looked at the quiet, composed face of the man beside her and said, "I think you were sent to me by heaven."

As I turn to the stable of Bethlehem where Jesus was born and to the cross where he died for our sins, I can say, "He was sent from heaven for me." To you he stands at your heart's door pleading, "Behold, I stand at the door, and knock: if any man hear my voice, and open the door, I will come in to him, and will sup with him and he with me."

14

The Saving of the Saved

"And the things that thou hast heard of me among many witnesses, the same commit thou to faithful men, who shall be able to teach others also" (2 Tim. 2:2).

We have majored on saving the lost but minored on "saving the saved." We have been busy making believers but failed to make disciples. It has been reported that last year more Baptists became nonresident members than were added to all our church rolls. If this continues, we face self-liquidation within a few years.

The Greek word for salvation embodies the thought of action which occurred in the past and is complete, but is also a progressive action which will continue indefinitely. Every Christian has been saved, is being saved, and will be saved. We must remain interested not only in the initial experience but likewise in the future experience of putting into living reality the whole duty of a believer.

A Baptist pastor relates the story of an experience on his grand-mother's farm. Late one afternoon she sent him out to coop the eight old hens. As he ran them through the door he counted them, all eight. To his surprise, he had nine, ten, and more. He discovered that a board was missing off the back of the coop, and the hens were getting out as fast as he put them in!

This story symbolizes the activity of the average church in the enlistment of its new members. Of the twelve and one-half million Baptists on the rolls of our churches, one-fourth are AWOL and not saved to the cause. Dr. Vance Havner quotes an old preacher who said, "Some have said that we need 'A Million More in '54' but if they are like the ones we already have, we are sunk." Every time we have a new convert added to the church we ought to have a new tither, a new Sunday School member, Church Training member, Brotherhood or WMU member and another attendant to all the services of the church. One of our leaders states that unless we enlist a new member within the first six weeks after he joins, he will probably never be enlisted.

The membership of our churches could be analyzed under several classifications of which I mention two. There is the division of three kinds: the *self-conscious* who have no clothes, the *self-sufficient* who have plenty of money and do not need the church, the *self-deceived* who think they are too busy to become active members of the church.

Another classification is a division of six kinds: First, the *growing in grace member,* who is faithful, dependable and loyal to the total program of the church. Daily he is becoming a stronger Christian as he grows in grace. Second, the *contemporary member* who lives by the standards of his associates. He lives no lower and yet no higher than the crowd with whom he associates. He drifts with what is current and popular. Third, the *difficult group* which contains those who are flagrant sinners who seek to hide their true nature and conduct from the church. They attempt to work themselves into responsible positions of the church, not in order to serve but to sever the fellowship of the church. It is this group which causes most of our problems and its members are perpetually hindering the program of God. The fourth is the *problem group.* They are sinners and know it. They want to find a solution to their problem and find power to live a victorious life. The fifth group consists of the *troubled.* The economic, social, and domestic problems of drunkenness, divorce, and discouragement plague them. The sixth group consists of the *down-and-outs.* They are the alcoholics, the ones in jail, and those generally turned down by society. It is the perennial task of the preacher to properly integrate these groups into one common brotherhood of a Christian community.

Sometime ago I read an article in a church bulletin which observed that nearly every modern businessman was supposed to have at least one ulcer. Several reasons were listed as being chiefly responsible—one was the labor problem, another was the keen competition, high overhead, and several other factors. When I read this article, I could not help thinking how many ulcers the poor businessman would have if he worked under the trying circumstances a pastor does.

Suppose, Mr. Businessman, you were overseer of almost 10,000 workers (about the membership of our church), suppose that only

50 percent of them ever showed up for work at any one time, and of the remaining 50 percent only about half of them with any degree of regularity.

Suppose that only one out of every ten of your workers showed up after lunch (our evening services), and every time one of them had a slight headache or company to visit them they "took off" that day. And every time it thundered or even a slight flash of lightning appeared in the sky 75 percent of your workers pulled the cover over their heads and never appeared for duty that day.

Suppose your workers only worked "when they felt like it," and still you must be sweet and never fire one of them. To induce them to work you beg them, plead with them, pat them on the head, pet them, tickle them under the chin, and use every means under the sun to cajole them into doing the work. And, suppose you were in competition with a notorious rascal (the devil) who had no scruples and was far more clever than you were and used such attractive lures as fishing rods, soft pillows, TV programs, ball games, parties, pleasure drives, and a thousand and one other things to hurt your business.

Suppose your firm was heavily obligated to meet certain financial responsibilities, and you had to depend upon your people to "give as they felt led" to carry out the biggest business in the world. So you think you have ulcers, Mr. Businessman! You ought to be in the shoes of a pastor for a while! Under God, Southern Baptists will undertake to do something about this tragic loss of human power which could be used to the glory of God!

We Ought to "Save" Them

It is the command of Jesus; "Teaching them to observe all things whatsoever I have commanded you" (Matt. 28:20).

Dr. E. D. Head said, "A person is not truly evangelized until he becomes an evangel." The Great Commission is an injunction to witness and train, to reach and teach, to save and serve. To be genuine the fruit must be reproductive.

The need of the individual prompts us to conserve him for service. The Bible likens a new Christian to a babe needing the attention of its parents. The church is often willing to rejoice in the birth but not in the responsibility of caring for growth. It appears that the accusation of the world concerning us is too often true. The world feels that we are interested in winning them to add to the church roll and have a larger membership, to be able to make an impressive report at the associational meeting, to secure more money for salaries and buildings, or merely to boost our egos. The real reason is because every soul outside of Jesus Christ is lost and going to hell, and woe is me if I preach not the gospel to them!

Many stay away because of denominational rivalries and bickering. Some dislike formal, elaborate rituals. And some (though they do not know it) follow the example of the noblest man our land has produced, Abraham Lincoln, who, in a startling and little-known statement of his faith, declared that he had never united with any church because he found difficulty in giving his assent, without mental reservations to the long, complicated statements of Christian doctrine which characterized articles of belief and confessions of faith.

This statement, even though there is no defense for his concept, reveals man's basic need of an experience of salvation and an outlet of expressive service through the New Testament Church. Modern times find us adopting the elements of Christianity which caused the period of the Dark Ages. In keeping alive the initial experience and joy of salvation, we must not permit expectancy to give way to complacency, or creeds to replace personal experience, or human manipulation to take the place of Holy Spirit action.

To save them is the hope of the future. We must save them for the sheer joy of it. Nothing saps the strength of the church like defeat from Satan. If God gives us a precious soul, we must make every effort to utilize that soul's every possibility to the glory of God. Every American takes delight in winning, whether it be in business, sports, or religion. There is a vibrant note in the life of a church which has the thrill of saving people. This spiritual experience overshadows any other earthly experience a Christian can have. To witness people being saved from sin, self, normalcy, and complacency to full service and dedication is a joy—it is a thrill!

We must save them for food. No other spiritual food will keep alive God's workers like winning victories against Satan and snatching souls and lives out of the sin of indifference. On the tidal wave of revival, in the midst of God's people, sweeps in the answer to every church problem. This is the solution to fellowship, discipleship, stewardship, and so forth. No church can grow which continues to add names to its roll but not lives to its ranks.

We ought to save them for funds. Every missionary on the field of service will be called home, every orphanage, hospital, seminary, and college will be closed, every church will have to tack up a sign on its front door, "For Sale," unless we save the additions and teach them to become good stewards of their possessions to continue the work of God. The church must save them so they can in turn save the church!

We Can Save Them

We have the helps. First, fellowship in our churches is the most wholesome to be found anywhere. The spirit of democracy among the saints presents a liberty and participation second to none. We ought to continue making this fellowship so vibrant and exciting that our members will be more loyal and faithful to our services than many are to their clubs and fraternities.

The second help is our facilities. No more are we simply a despised sect shoved off into some obscure area of the city in a dilapidated one-room building. Today our mighty church plants stand in the most prominent places in most of our cities. Millions of dollars have been invested in worship centers, educational departments, and recreational facilities as available instruments to save our people from going back into a life with the world. Today as never before the church ought to provide a seven-day-a-week program that will meet every phase of complex life—socially, mentally, physically, and religiously.

Our hindrances are many. The caste system in American life, as expressed in social and financial differences, poses a problem of proper integration of new members. By preaching and practicing the equality of believers in Christ, we can overcome this feeling of being unwelcome on the part of members.

A selfish, egocentric attitude on the part of members causes them to lack a personal interest in other people. This creates a feeling of intrusion in the minds of new converts if they are placed in this environment.

One of the chief hindrances is the fact that the church doesn't see the ultimate worth of the individual to the kingdom of God and thus, ignores its opportunity to help in the development of new babes in Christ.

We will "save the saved" if we help them to understand what happened at conversion and how God now indwells them in the Holy Spirit to make possible a victorious life. Jesus must become real to them if they are to continue in their commitment. They must understand the continued work of God through his Spirit.

The work of the Holy Spirit is first to the unbeliever convicting of "sin, and of righteousness, and of judgment" (John 16:8). He enters into the life at conversion and baptizes a person into the body of Jesus Christ (Gal. 3:27 and Rom. 6:3).

We have all received the baptism of the Holy Spirit at conversion and become one in and with Jesus Christ. Now we have his nature which is unchanging forever. Since Ephesians 4:4-6 declares there is but one baptism, this experience is not to be repeated after a person recieves Christ. Many persons think that the baptism of the Spirit is a special experience reserved for certain priviledged people and a few of God's greatest. This is not true, and the Bible teaches that this grace is open to all believers. In fact, Paul says that we cannot be Christians without the Holy Spirit, "Now if any man have not the Spirit of Christ, he is none of his" (Rom. 8:9).

Far too many Christians confuse "baptism" and "filling." They hunger and thirst for a new experience with God, because their lives are empty of happiness and peace. This is a desire for the filling of his Spirit. Fullness is a willingness to surrender to him who is now in your life. We can't receive more of him, but he can receive more of us as we yield our lives to him.

The newborn babe in Christ must now recognize that he cannot live the Christian life and if he tries will fail. He must understand that only Jesus can do that and he will in and through the Christian. The believer must be controlled by the Spirit of God.

Once the Holy Spirit baptizes an individual into the body of Christ, he then equips the believer for service by giving him gifts of the Spirit. Approximately nineteen different gifts are listed in the Bible, and every Christian has one or more of these endowments. All the gifts are given by the selection of the Spirit to equip the members of the body of Christ to fulfill God's purpose in reconciling the world to him. These gifts are not given to edify self but are to be humbly received and given to the body of Christ, the church.

The many gifts available to the surrendered Christian are listed in 1 Corinthians 12:4,8-10,28. They are as follows: The gifts of wisdom, knowledge, faith, healing, working miracles, prophecy, discerning spirits, tongues, interpretation of tongues, apostleship, teaching, giving assistance, governing, the gift of being evangelists, pastors, and liberality.

There is a new emphasis on the person and work of the Holy Spirit. This is giving churches a fresh heavenly experience which is producing supernatural experiences. We all favor God doing his mighty work in today's world. The secret of this aliveness, excitement, and new joy is the result of Christians discovering their spiritual gifts and using them in the service of our Lord. The task of the spiritual leadership in our fellowship is to help believers find and use their special gifts in the task of service.

15

The Hell of Hells

"The wicked shall be turned into hell, and all the nations that forget God" (Ps. 9:17).

Many church people in these modern times do not believe in a literal hell. If we did accept the biblical teaching on the subject, we would be motivated to be urgent in our witnessing to the lost. If one does not believe this doctrine, he will need to debate it with Jesus because most of what we know about the subject came from his lips.

A minister once remarked in a reaction to my sermons, "We do not attempt to scare people into religion by preaching on hell. We do not believe in hell; however, if you read the New Testament you will notice that Jesus mentioned it several times."

It is not strange that today many deny outright the doctrine of hell. Some speak against this truth apologetically or with qualifications to subdue its aspects of eternal punishment. The question in our minds today is the "why" of this questioning among Christian people. What is the purpose of such a message? What do we hope to derive from it? Why should we deal with the subject of hell at all?

First—This is a Bible doctrine, and there is an increasing interest on the part of our people for Bible truth. They are asking as never before, "What saith the Lord?" Our preaching has settled down to a compromise between the Puritan extreme of one and one-half hour sermons and the modern-day fifteen minute devotional period of "do-it-yourself" religion, to a demand on the part of our congregations for a message of doctrine from the World of God.

Dr. Havner tells the story of a young preacher who spoke to a group of rural folks, and when he had finished, he asked one of the old-timers what he thought of his sermon. The old man replied quickly, "I didn't think much of it." "But why?" inquired the young theological student. Looking the preacher straight in the eye the old man said: "Because there has been a lack of emphasis on the doctrine of hell today because of a theological reaction against the school of Jonathan Edwards who magnified the subject in his masterful sermon 'Sinners in the Hands of an Angry God.' " Our reaction has caused an emphasis on the love of God as explained in the New Testament. We forget that the love of God is conditional. John 3:16 is full of the love of God, but is also full of condemnation and wrath. There are two sides to every coin and one is as realistic as the other.

Second—We need to stand in apostolic tradition in our position of preaching this doctrine. These men were intimately associated with Christ and consequently knew his mind and soul. If they, having been taught by him, preached this doctrine, then so should we. Here is what they have said:

Peter speaks, "He seeing this before spake of the resurrection of Christ, that his soul was not left in hell" (see Acts 2:31).

James speaks, "The tongue is set on fire of hell" (see Jas. 3:6).

John speaks, "And whosoever was not found written in the book of life was cast into a lake of fire" (see Rev. 20:15).

Third—Old truths need to be recast and restated to modern minds. Great principles never change but methods do. Man's nature doesn't change but approach to men's minds vary. If a man goes to Africa and finds little children playing with semiround rocks but later discovers that they are diamonds in the rough, it could change the economy of that nation. The value and worth of an individual soul is determined by the truth concerning hell as a reality.

Now let us look at Psalm 9:17: "The wicked shall be turned into hell, and all the nations that forget God." This verse notes two classifications of people who will enter hell: the wicked and forgetful. It is easy to understand how certain people like wicked harlots, murderers, and drunkards, would go to hell, but it is hard for us to understand and believe how some "good" people who merely forget God will go to hell.

Jesus' Description of Hell

Jesus said that hell was a place of torment (Luke 16:19-31). Theologians through the ages have debated with hair-splitting accuracy whether this torment suggested by Jesus is literal or figurative. Space does not permit us to discuss the two aspects of this age-long question; but suffice it to say that if we are able to prove it to be figurative, we do not solve the problem but only compound it. We compound our problem because a figure of speech is an accomodation to place in the area of human experience that which is impossible to understand otherwise.

To illustrate such we ask the question, "Have you ever been up in a space ship or can you imagine the thrilling experience of going into outer space?" Your reply, of course, would most likely be in the negative. Then I would attempt to explain by accomodation so that we could relate this experience of going into outer space in a space ship to something with which you are acquainted. To explain my point I would talk about the feeling you had when you rode in your first roller coaster or your first trip on a jet. My point in hand would be that these experiences are miniature examples of what you would feel if you were to fly in a space ship. In like manner, any symbolic language of the New Testament which describes hell means to reflect a more terrible ordeal in the actual experience to come.

The hell of hells involves some torments far more intense than the sufferings of a life affected by literal fire. Here is the picture of a mother dying with lung cancer. Her son is a wayward, lost drunkard who took her insurance money, left her after her husband's death, and has abandoned her in poverty to die. She on her deathbed is praying for his salvation. This spiritual pain is worse than physical pain. A fine Christian woman in our community saw her son get into trouble and end up in the state penitentiary. The day he was removed from the local jail, I stood in her home for prayer and later heard her sob, "Pastor, this hurts me worse than death." These are some torments worse than those effecting the physical body. The language of Jesus, literal or figurative—the hell of hells is terrible.

The Real Hell

The real hell of hells has involved in it more aspects and characteristics than mere physical suffering from fire. To be true that probably is one aspect but not all. At one time, we thought light was only one color, white. One day the sun cast the rays through a prism and reflected itself on the wall and revealed seven colors:

red, orange, yellow, green, blue, indigo, and violet. Hell casts itself through the prism of the Bible and reflects itself on the minds of men to reveal all the varied aspects of the suffering of hell.

1. One aspect of a real hell is separation from God which includes separation from light, love, and life. Revelation 20:14 reads, "And death and hell were cast into the lake of fire." Death means separation which comes in the first death and spiritual separation in this life and hereafter. The Scriptures affirm that if we have not received Christ, we are now dead in our sins. The sentence of death is not just on us but is written in us. Eternal life is inherent and salvation begins now—not at death or in heaven, and it is even so with hell. A non-Christian is already condemned, already separated from God and even so, in a sense, has begun his state of living in hell. Thus saith the Scripture, "And in hell he lifted up his eyes being in torment" (Luke 16:23).

2. Another aspect of hell is its utter hopelessness and helplessness. As Dante expressed in *The Divine Comedy*, "All hope abandon, ye who enter here." There is no hope for escape, peace of body and mind, or forgiveness. This is the final end for all who reject the gospel.

A man in prison was asked by an evangelist who spoke there, "How long are you in for?" Pathetically he replied, "That is just it— forever." The hopelessness of it. A man was in a mental hospital. One day a friend came in for a brief visit with hopes of encouraging the patient. The visitor said, "You are not to become discouraged; we all get depressed." "Yes," replied the patient, "you can talk like that because you can leave any time you want, but I can't." The hopelessness of it.

A man was working in an underground sewer, and it caved in on him. For forty-eight hours he was trapped beneath six feet of dirt with certain death staring him in the face. Oh, what he must have thought! How he must have suffered. However, none of this physical pain was too bad if only he could have hope of escape. Men would suffer any physical pain to gain escape from hell, but there is none. The hell of hells is the hopelessness of escape.

Dr. R. G. Lee says, "Hell is a place from which there are no exits." In public halls, in bold letters, you will see EXIT. But no sign like that in hell, once there, always there. Once in, never out.

Jesus says, "Great gulf fixed." Impassable to those who would come from there, here. Open your eyes and look before you enter a place from which no man has ever returned—a place where those who enter come not out forever, but lift up wailing voices to warn those who are wise enough to hear and heed.

Hell is a place of retribution. Hebrews 2:2 speaks of this: "For if the word spoken by angels was stedfast, and every transgression and disobedience received a just recompence of reward . . ." Abraham reminds us of this unalterable fact, "Son, remember that thou in thy lifetime receivedst thy good things" (Luke 16:25). What did he remember? Opportunity, invitations, sermons, influence?

Memory manifests its greatest punishment to us by creating a sense of justice. In hell a person is not in indecision as to his just punishment, but he realizes that he is to blame for this eternal consequence.

In one of the major cities of our state, a newspaper carried this true story. A woman through the years mistreated and abused her husband until in final despair he committed suicide. At the funeral and since then, she has been going around in a daze crying: "I did it . . . I did it! I could have prevented it. It is all my fault. I am to blame for what happened!" The hell of hells causes remorse from a sense of God's justice expressed in our punishment.

God doesn't so much punish us *for* our sins but *by* our sins, in time and eternity. We remember the goodness of God, the prevailing invitations, our constant refusal to yield our lives to him. A while back a young man discussed his problem with me. Several years ago he felt God wanted him to preach and so he enrolled in one of our Baptist colleges. After two years of study and preparation, he decided he had made a mistake. His reaction to this experience led him into a life of sinful pleasures, where he went down and down spiritually. After several years of this type of living, which only led to unhappiness, he repented and was restored to fellowship with God. He continued to be unhappy because as he remembered his sinful life he was so ashamed until he said, "I feel so dirty—having done these terrible things." He suffered in his sins in the retention of memory and so will every person who goes to hell.

Here is a place of spiritual zeal and missionary concern (Luke 16:27-28). The rich man in hell was more concerned about his brothers than many nominal Christians today. He really believed in hell as a place of punishment and was interested in warning others to avoid it. The average church member doesn't believe with the same passion as the rich man. This is evidenced by our lack of soul-winning passion and our pittance of gifts to missions. The lost world today is not convinced; men have failed to repent of their sins and turn to the "Lamb of God, which taketh away the sin of the world."

Hope of Escape in Christ Through Repentance

We would be the last ones to argue that Christianity is a mere fire escape from perdition; nevertheless, we must admit that this aspect is true. Always the antithesis of hell is heaven and to escape one assures the gain of the other. Man will be encouraged to flee the eternal punishment of hell if we make plain and lucid the way of escape.

The judgment of God is his expression of wrath *against sin* and *not the sinner*. Many have the wrong concept of God's wrath. God is not an angry despot sitting in the heavens with a telescope turned upon man ready to punish the least infraction of the law.

Rather, the wrath of God is this . . . God has made physical and spiritual laws, and these cannot be disregarded without a subsequent reaction. Newton proved the law of gravity which is God's creation in physical law. If a man attempts to defy this law by jumping off the church building, he hurts himself: he cannot destroy the law but will destroy himself. God has made spiritual laws, and man destroys himself by attempting to defy God's revealed laws and will which is based on the love of God.

William Elbert Munsey has stated in more graphic words than mine this picture:

"Sin is an immense river running through secret channels from Hell's seething ocean, till it broke out upon this world in the Garden of Eden. There at the foot of the tree of knowledge of good and evil is its source . . . noisy spring bubbling with the escape of baneful gases, in whose tenebrious depths a serpent lives. Ever enlarging, this river flows all around the world. Onward it sweeps. Upon its banks no flowers grow, no foliage waves, but perpetual desolation pitches its pavillions upon the sterile strand, relieved here and there by bald and scoriac rocks, upon which weeping spirits sit and curse the day that they were born. In all the universe there is no river so wide, so deep, so swift as this. Its floods are black, its waves are towering, and it goes surging and roaring on to the bottomless lake, everlasting lightnings pencilling every billowy crest with angry fire, and Hell's terrific thunders bounding from bank to bank and bursting with awful crash and strewing dread ruin all around.

"Surely such a river might roll on forever unvisited by mortal man. But oh, alas! Climax of all wonders! Quintessence of all marvels! Its shores are lined from source to mouth with human wretches. They crowd to gain its edges, all sexes, all conditions, all classes. The mother decks her daughter's brow, and side by side they leap into the boisterous flood. Into its boiling current the young maiden runs laughing, and passes from sight in a moment; the old man following, his locks streaming in the wind like the shredded canvas of a storm-ridden ship reeling upon the foamy summit of a stupendous wave that washes heaven, but to be hurled the next moment by the driving blast into the raging vortex below, and be swallowed up forever. Between every human being and this fearful river there is a bleeding body and a bloody cross, and angels positioned on every height and hovering over every head and shouting, 'Stop! In the name of God, pause for a moment.' But disregarding the angelic warning and trampling upon both body and cross, with gory feet they spring far out into the murky tide and join their fellows until every wave is freighted and instinct with human souls, and all together carried onward and in one eternal roar poured over the boundaries of human probation into Acheron's fiery sea, forced downward by the plunging floods to perdition's deepest dungeons, to rise far out from shore upon flaming waves unquenchable, to scream forever with unmitigated and ceaseless woe."

16

Holy Spirit Power

There is a renewed emphasis today on the doctrine of the Holy Spirit. This is one of the most refreshing signs of our day and has brought new life to many apathetic churches. As is always true, there are some errors accompanying this activity of God in the believer and church of today's world.

Some people who are members of cold, dead, formal churches are hearing about the Holy Spirit for the first time and are being saved. Others are making in-depth commitments and are being filled with the Spirit. Many are in confusion as to gifts and ministries, thus creating problems in some fellowships. A pressing need today is biblical preaching on the person, power, and program of the Holy Spirit.

A pastor in a large denomination stated recently, "I believe that the Holy Spirit has been withdrawn from the world because we are no longer having conviction of sin or revival." One of our leading Southern Baptist Convention pastors said that if the Holy Spirit departed from us, at least 95 percent of what we are doing as a church would go on as usual. I would agree with the latter statement but cannot accept the first, because the Scriptures and experience attest to the real presence of God in his Spirit.

The church in today's world is like the basketball referee who was standing with whistle in mouth when some spectator slapped him on the back and caused him to accidently swallow the whistle. He is now going around coughing and sputtering, neither able to stop the game nor to direct the activity. The church is like that in our world; neither able to change the direction of lost men or stop the action of resistance to the gospel. Our only explanation is our failure to appropriate the personal power of the Holy Spirit.

I am convinced that a continous study of this doctrine will give a new perspective to any believer and runs the risk of bringing spiritual revolution to him.

There are two basic Scriptures which launch our study, Acts 1:8 and Acts 19:2. In the first passage we are promised power— "dynamite"—when the Holy Ghost is come upon us. All the power the church or the believer needs is available in him if we can understand and appropriate this truth.

Many of us are like the disciples from Ephesus who were asked of Paul, "Have you received the Holy Ghost since you believed?" (Acts 19:2). Their reply in a spirit of doubt was, "We have not so much as heard whether there be any Holy Ghost."

If you ask the average church member if he has received the baptism and filling of the Holy Ghost, he simply shrugs his shoulders and states that he didn't know we believed in a baptism of the Holy Spirit. There is no wonder that we are powerless in our lives and churches, when we have so neglected the work of his Spirit in our presence. Then it becomes imperative that we understand his Person, power, and program in our contemporary world.

Why Study This Subject?

Our total dependence is upon him. No one can be saved without him, for he must convict of sin. There is no Christian growth without him, for he sanctifies the believer. Prayers are never answered without him, for he interprets our petitions to the Father. A reader cannot understand the Bible without him, for he who gave us Scripture by inspiration must so interpret it to us now. You can't preach, teach, witness, sing, or do any other spiritual ministry without him. We are totally dependent upon him to make any human effort effective.

We must study this doctrine, because the Bible makes reference to him over 378 times in the Old Testament and 335 times in the New Testament. Any subject mentioned as often as the Holy Spirit must be of supreme importance.

Conditions of the world today necessitate our dependence upon some power beyond ourselves. The war, crime, hate, lust, and immorality of our times reminds us of our inadequacy to solve our problems. There must be a divine encounter with the supernatural Being who has all power to overcome these existing circumstances. God alone, who is the Creator, can conquer and change man's rebellious nature, and this he is working to do in and through his Spirit. We have hope today because the Holy Spirit assures us that he is a restrainer of sin and will not permit sin to completely engulf this world. In Isaiah 59 there is the picture of God's Spirit raising a standard against the tidal wave of sin and stopping its conquest. There will always be God's remnant in whom his Spirit will continue to work until the coming of their King . . . Jesus Our Lord.

The condition of the church today makes it imperative that we return to an emphasis of the Holy Spirit. We have the form but have denied the power of God by his Spirit. We are maintaining the status quo: business as usual, but no real depth commitment. It has been a long time since we have experienced the unexplainable moving of God in our midst to convict sinners of their need of repentance. How long has it been since you heard a heart sob of concern in a service? When did you last become caught up in a mighty tidal wave of supernatural, Pentecostal power of the Spirit? Churches have so neglected him until they continue their routine but without his presence or blessing.

When there is apparent neglect of teaching on this subject, then rationalism, which is destructive criticism, moves in. There is a denial of the supernatural, the deity of Christ, and the inspiration of Scripture. Ritualism moves into the churches and becomes a substitute for the real presence of God in his Spirit. Human nature, having a desire to worship, substitutes that which is sensual and appeals to our senses. The less of his Spirit, the more human elements and forms become the absolute in our worship experience. Modern man tries to build his towers of Babel which makes self the center rather than God.

Why We Have Neglected This Doctrine

Splendid material and numerical gains within our churches during the past few years have given us the pride of success. We believe that anything we want can be achieved if we organize and promote it in the right manner. There is no child-like dependence on God when man feels adequate. In recent years we have lost our cutting edge no longer penetrating society as once we did, and as an article in a news magazine stated, the churches are in trouble. There is no trouble which we face that cannot be resolved by a return to the biblical view of the ministry of the Holy Spirit.

Strength in the organizational church led us to find security in our relationship to a large, popular, apparently successful, denomination. We boast of our size, numbers, and accomplishments and feel that we can never fall because of our attachment to the giant structure.

There is a new sense of security because now we generally are the accepted group. We have moved from the backwoods to the boulevard. The best people in our city now belong to our fellowship. No longer are we the despised sect, located on the other side of the tracks. Perhaps we need more persecution and punishment to make our faith cost.

A wave of pseudo-intellectualism has swept into our pulpits and pews denouncing any sign of emotionalism. Our people live in a world of emotionalism with television soap operas and sports until they are drained of any capacity to respond with heart in a worship experience. The pulpit advocates an intellectual approach to spiritual things void of emotional expressions. Often we are now gathering in little groups at eleven o'clock Sunday morning preaching little sermonettes to members hopped up on tranquilizers without capacity for concern or praise.

Why This Apparent Ignorance?

We are ignorant of the source of authority for this doctrine—the Bible. One can never grasp this truth until he is willing to acquaint himself with the Word of God. If you want to know about relativity you read Newton, or anatomy you read Graves, or medicine, you read Cecil, or law you read Blackstone. If you would know more about the Holy Spirit, you must search for him in the Word of God. Because we are ignorant of the Bible, we are ignorant of the Holy Spirit.

Some translations of Scripture mislead many believers. In Romans 8:26 there is the usage, "the Spirit itself," giving the impression that the Holy Spirit is neuter rather than masculine. The Greek language permits the usage of the neuter noun when referring to a person but it confuses many. All references in both Testaments mention him as a person with God the Father and Christ the Son—and the Holy Spirit. He is not an atmosphere or influence, as we shall later study, but a person as other members of the godhead.

The term "Ghost" gives a wrong connotation to many who think in terms of spooks, hallowe'en, pranks, and the like. Really, the word ghost is derived from the same meaning of the word guest. God, in his Spirit, is then the Holy Guest of our lives who comes to dwell with us. When a guest comes, we prepare to be our best and place at his disposal every available possession. We can do no less for the Holy Spirit when he enters our lives to reside with us.

We have permitted some fanatical groups to scare us away from the truth. They have said to us, "We have the Holy Spirit and you do not because we manifest it in emotional extravaganza and tongues." We have reacted by assuming that if this is the activity of the Holy Spirit, we want none of it. Because of our position, we have leaned over backward to a point of extreme and become the greater loser. I can go along with any crowd who overemphasizes this doctrine better than I can go with a cold, dead, liturgical group which is empty and dead. Somewhere between these two extremes is the biblical truth we must understand and apply.

Our greatest reason for ignorance is our practice of substituting church activity for the work of the Spirit. We say that a person is filled with the Spirit when he is busy in church work. I must remind you that there is nothing we are doing in religious activity that any lost person could not do in the flesh. The difference comes in the power of God present in the believer's life to make the work effective. You can be busy, busy, busy in church work and not be controlled by the Holy Spirit, but you can't be filled with the Spirit and not be busy. Too much that we are doing is in the flesh rather than the Spirit which explains the lack of joy, happiness, and fulfillment in the lives of our busy church workers.

A black preacher visited the tomb of John Wesley. As he stood silently by, he remembered how God had used Wesley to move two nations closer to heaven, and how the Spirit of God had moved upon sinners for conversion. He removed his hat, knelt at the tomb, and with tears streaming down his cheeks, cried in prayer, "Do it again, Lord, do it again!"

17

Faith in Times Like These

Job is one of the most fascinating books of the Bible, one which has stirred the imagination of Bible scholars and literary giants. We do not know the author, the man Job, or the place of Uz. Perhaps it is best because all mankind is represented in this experience of human suffering and man's struggle to find meaning and purpose in it. Many believe that the book of Job is the oldest book of the Bible, written before any other part of the Old Testament. It is about a man in whom God and Satan are interested.

Dr. John R. Sampey has noted that the only way we can fully understand Job's difficulty is to realize his limited revelation of the nature and promises of God. He had no assurance of God's provision as we have throughout the Word of God. And he had no revelation of God as we understand him in Jesus Christ. We must also remember that everything written in Job is not true. We have statements made by Satan, Job's friends, and even Job which are not true, and God corrects these misunderstandings. For instance, God says to Eliphaz, "My wrath is kindled against thee, and against thy two friends: for ye have not spoken of me the thing that is right, as my servant Job hath" (Job 42:7).

There has been some discussion whether Job was a historical character or merely a parable teaching a truth. We must accept the thesis that it is historically true because he is referred to in Ezekiel along with Noah (Ezek. 14:14-20), and in James 5:11, and these passages establish that Job really lived and suffered and was victorious.

The book was written as poetry and the action is that of a dramatic presentation. In fact, Broadway featured a play called *J. B.* for several years. It was clearly based on the predicament of Job.

The scene of Job begins with Job on earth with his prosperity and blessings and in chapter 3 it moves to heaven where Satan accuses

Job before God. Alexander Whyte referred to this as is the greatest debate of all times.

Out of this struggle, questions are asked, questions which no man can fully answer; but Jesus has given the answer and we shall find them in our studies. We begin with a study of the man, Job.

The Character of Job

Job was an ideal man in that he faced every tragic experience of mankind and in them all he was steadfast to God in his faith. These are the qualities of character which we should possess to live in today's world with all its problems and frustrations. Let us look at the remarks the Bible makes concerning Job.

He was perfect and upright. The word "perfect" in the Hebrew language did not means sinless perfection, because Job admits that he was a sinner. Rather, "perfect" signified "complete." In other words, Job's life manifested the complete qualities which were necessary for Job to live uprightly. The term had to do with his outward character of honesty, integrity, and trustworthy dependability. The description "complete" has to do with his inner life and "upright" has to do with his outward life.

Job feared God in his life. The idea is not that Job lived in constant dread of his God but rather that he set the will of God before him as his rule of life. More than anything, it was Job giving consideration to God in every aspect of existence. Contrary to that relationship to God, modern man often lives as if there were no God, and consequently his total existence is one of despair.

He eschewed evil all of his life. This means that he shunned all sin and even the very appearance of it. Job revealed this attitude in his home by having a family altar where he and his family constantly worshiped God and kept out of his home every suggestion of evil. When he went into the courts of men to do business, he reflected in all his transactions integrity and honesty.

Happiness was one of his chief assets. He is seen constantly rejoicing along with his family over the blessings of God. His happiness was built on the principle that even though he had everything, he really had nothing. His happiness was not dependent on things, for he can be seen rejoicing at the end of the experience even as he was in the beginning. Job proves that happiness cannot be found by searching but rather is an inner experience of relationship with God.

The Conflicts of Job

Every imaginable problem confronted the man Job. He constantly struggled with conflicts but in the end was victorious over them, not in his power but in the power of God in his life. What were these conflicts?

Satan accused him before God and claimed that Job served God only for the things he could get out of it. He questioned Job's motive for being religious and was given permission by God to put Job to the ultimate test. Remember that the devil can never do to us anymore than God will permit. Many calamities which befall us must be the works of Satan.

Temptation to deny God came when Job was prosperous. Finally, he lost every earthly possession. He was the wealthiest man in Uz, and it was embarrassing to a successful businessman to lose every material possession he owned. This is always the test of true character and faith in God. If a man is faking his faith in God, it will be evident when he loses his fortune. True faith in God will not always explain why things happen but will give grace to accept the teaching of Romans 8:28, "All things work together for good to them that love God."

There is nothing more depressing than sickness. When a person's body is racked with disease it is difficult to be spiritual. God can see us through sickness and make us stronger because of it. Suffering can draw us closer to God or drive us away in doubt. Our response to it determines the end result.

Job's wife misunderstood and recommended that Job give up and curse God. She was not advocating that he junk God and become irreverent to him but rather that she would prefer to see Job dead than suffer like that. We have seen our loved ones go through such pain that we have thought, This is too much, I would rather see them go to be with the Lord.

Job's friends are not to be condemned unduly because their analysis of his problems of suffering was based on the Jewish concept that all suffering was due to sin in the sufferer's life. His friends are to be commended because of their faithfulness in visiting him and

their willingness to sit silently for days. But his friends were comfortless to him in his hour of need, and he was left alone in his
misery. It is hard to see your close friends no longer standing by
in understanding, but blaming you for your trouble.

Job's greatest problem was his own inner struggle of his soul.
Doubts and questions confounded Job as he sought for meaning in
this experience. Finally, he saw the answer but it came after the
"dark night of the soul."

Conviction of Job

We can learn from every experience if we will walk with God.
To rebel against the circumstances of life and complain means we
miss the good which can come from trying experiences.

Job realized that without God he was nothing, for he states, "Naked
I came into the world." He did what everyone should. He realized
that God owned everything and that he was only a steward of God's
possessions. This truth will determine all mankind's attitude to possessions.

He had every material advantage a man could possess yet was
not dependent on these things for happiness. When with one stroke
of providence all was taken from him, it did not delete his happiness,
for he said, "Even though he slay me, yet will I trust in him."

Job understood that even though he could not fully comprehend
the events in his life, God was in charge. He knew God was there,
for his plea was to find him. Modern man should know that all
history is filled with the presence of God and that he is working
within all experiences to fulfill his divine purpose.

The greatest conviction which came out of his suffering was that
he could still have faith in troubled times. Faith in God is contemporary and relevant in everyday life. Too many people accuse us
of an interest by and by and no emphasis on the now. When Karl
Marx came on the scene, he asserted, in essence, "Christianity is
only promising you pie in the sky by and by but communism will
give it to you now."

We are interested in eternal life beyond this human existence,
but the faith we have relates to every human experience. What does
the Christian faith give in this troubled world? First, pardon from

our sin. This relieves the guilt of our rebellion against the God who created and loves us. It gives us peace in times of unhappiness. Weary men should come to God through Jesus Christ. Last of all, it gives us power to live the kind of life our better selves want us to live. In reality, it is *his life lived through us.*

To become a person of faith, one must come to Christ for forgiveness knowing that God loves him and will receive him gladly.

18

The World's Only Hope

One Wednesday morning Dr. Warren Hultgren called me and with excited emotion said, "Turn your television on. Robert F. Kennedy has been shot." With all other Americans, I joined in shock and sadness at this grim tragedy and watched and prayed during the critical hours that followed.

It seems that news commentators, politicians, clergymen, and people at large tried to analyze the event but no one could give a sure answer. Statements ran wild about a controlled gun law, the need of men to quit hating, and the possible need of a stronger presidential control bordering on dictatorship. No one to whom I listened even touched on the spiritual need of man or our nation. This is the problem, and its only solution is a return to God.

The revolution seen in America reaches beyond to France, Italy, Indonesia, and almost every nation on the face of the earth. Billy Graham said it looks as if the devil has turned loose his demons, and they are taking over in the world where we live. For the first time in many years, our leaders are admitting the involvement of Communistic forces in Southeast Asia, college campuses, and even in our government. This passion and force of evil is anti-Christian and can only be overcome by the presence and power of God. However, we are still looking for a solution without turning to God.

America and the world is simply reaping what we have sown. We have said the church is irrelevant, the gospel inadequate, God is the opiate of the people, and Jesus Christ is unnecessary. We have gone the way of the liberals, humanists, secularists, and materialists. There is a decline in our belief in God and an exodus from the church. The Word of God has been ruled from our schools. Public prayer in education is prohibited. We have left the general impression to our family and friends that we don't need God. What is the end result? Revolution and havoc.

Billy Graham has traveled around the world and talked with most great leaders and they are all pessimistic about a solution. They have given up hope of working things out and bringing about peace and order.

As Dr. J. W. Storer, former president of the Southern Baptist Convention said: We as Christians cannot be optimists in the light of what is happening in the world. We cannot be pessimists even though the world has fallen to pieces. As Christians we are "hopist," for we believe that Jesus Christ is our sure hope. This is true, for 1 John 3:3 clearly states, "And every man that hath this hope in him purifieth himself, even as he is pure." Then, our only hope is not in social reform but in a spiritual renewal which the New Testament calls regeneration of man and society.

The Object of Our Hope

The believer today can have hope because we do not look mainly for a millennium, a rapture, a tribulation, *but for him.* Jesus Christ whom God has appointed as Savior of this world is also to be its judge—he is coming to receive his church, the bride, and reject those who rejected him.

He is to be the world's hope. Philosophers, theologians, scientists, and reformers have tried to give us hope, but it has all failed. It is like the blind leading the blind. Examples are evidences of what I declare.

Plato in his *Republic* envisioned a world run by philosophers who would usher in Utopia for us. This has failed, for educational achievement without Jesus Christ only equips the devil to a more devilish devil!

Aristotle saw humanity coming to a place of ideal brotherhood where all men would live in peace. This is utterly impossible, for men cannot be brothers until they all make God their Father. As long as God is rejected and ignored, there will be no common brotherhood of man.

Augustine, the great Catholic theologian, wrote *The City of God* in which he envisioned the institutional church bringing in peace and order. We know that the church is no dispenser of salvation but rather a proclaimer of "good news" about faith in Jesus Christ.

H. G. Wells stated that science will usher in an era of peace and tranquility. After two thousand years since Christ, science has made steady progress but man has not developed spiritually. We have seen slogans, marches, and legislation and none of this has produced peace. I can understand man's longing for peace but I can't understand his looking for it in the wrong direction. He is creation's hope. Romans 8:22 notes, "For we know that the whole creation groaneth and travaileth in pain together until now." The Bible teaches that even nature expresses its lack of perfection. The storm, hurricane, disease, and all dangers to mankind need to be conquered to fulfill God's original purpose, but it can only happen in his coming. He is the creation's hope.

He is the Jew's hope. There is no people in history who have been more misunderstood and mistreated than the Jew. They have been hated, and despised over the earth. Hitler alone murdered over six million Jews. God has some purpose with his chosen people, even though we can't fully understand now. They have a nation but this is not Israel's hope, its hope is the coming of Christ.

Jesus is the Christian's hope. Our text states in 1 John 3:2, "We shall see him." Yes, we shall see him and be like him. This is the constant struggle and goal of the believer—to be like him and yet we are unable until we see him in his glory. Our hope then to become what our hearts desire is to see him. The Bible talks more about his coming than any other subjects, such as repentance, faith, baptism, or other major doctrines. The Old Testament predicted the coming of Jesus. In the New Testament, Jesus affirmed it in statements and symbols. The two ordinances of the church, the Lord's Supper and baptism, depict his coming. Everything we believe or do should have in mind the coming of our Lord as our hope.

The Basis of Our Hope

The apostles believed in the coming of Christ, and so should every Christian today. In fact, as we study God's Word, he gives us signs of his coming which remind us the time is near. Some of these are apparent.

There are mental signs. The Bible tells us at the time of his coming men will have great fear in their hearts. This causes an emotional disorder and often leads to suicide. Over one-half of all hospital beds today are filled with people who have mental rather than physical problems.

There are moral signs: violence, murder, and sadism flourish, and one of the contributing factors is our own field of entertainment. The average American family watches television five-and-one-half hours daily. The liquor industry, the pornographic pushers, the lewd pictures give us a distorted view of life which we imitate. Eric Sevareid on his commentary concerning the death of our national leaders said that we are reaping what we have sown in publishing books like Mickey Spillane's where guns and violence are given credence. Even the toy industry has majored on destructive ideas rather than helpful.

There are spiritual signs, a falling away from the church, a revolt to the ministry, a decline in membership, and an apostasy even in the clergy. Our own theological leaders have pronounced the death of God and irrelevance of the church. The Word of God reminds us that men would have itching ears wanting to hear nice things about themselves but reject the true Word from God.

There are signs of violence. "Wars and rumors of wars" is the prophecy from Scriptures such as Matthew 24:7, "For nation shall rise against nation, and kingdom against kingdom: and there shall be famines, and pestilences, and earthquakes in divers places." Ammunition factories produced war materials and shipped them to all parts of the world, thus arming nations as never before. Russia developed a missile which can travel around the earth in outer space and can be released on America any time she desires. This is a frightful prospect . . . total destruction of mankind. Sociologists predict that in spite of all that nations can do, multiplied millions of people will starve because of the population explosion. All this is but God's sign of the coming of Christ.

The Proof of Our Hope

The proof of our personal hope is the fact that we are constantly being purified to become like him in character and nature. As Jesus was pure so ought the hope of his coming make us like him. Jesus told three stories and used these analogies to help us live the Christian life in light of his coming. In these three stories are found three key words.

The first is *watch.* The believer is to live a life of expectancy watching for the coming of his Lord. If a child knows his father is coming home after a long absence, he will want to clean up and be ready for his appearance. The believer will do likewise if he has the real hope in his heart.

The second word is *occupy*. Jesus told his followers to be occupied until he comes. This doesn't mean to keep the status quo, or to sit upon in defense. The word used means "to trade with." In Jesus' words, we were to be busy working, trading, enlarging his kingdom until he comes. There is nothing I would rather be doing when he comes than trying to build his kingdom and church.

The third word is *ready*. Before the coming of our Lord, he said we are *to be* ready, not to get ready, for when he comes—we will not have time to get ready. His coming will be like lightning flashing across the sky. Light travels at 186,000 miles a second, and if Jesus' coming is faster than that men won't have time to get ready. So be ready! All men want to be ready to meet God but we delay our preparation until it is too late.

When Robert Kennedy was shot, the first thing that was done was to put a crucifix in his hand. His prestige, education, wealth, his family all suddenly became secondary matters. Then it was a matter of what he could do to prepare to meet God. This is the eternal question you must face, for until you do you have no hope. In 2 Thessalonians 1:7-9 the Scripture indicates there are two classes of people who have no hope, those who know not God and those who obey not the gospel.

There is hope for the sinner. If you are lonely, defeated, and heavy hearted, you can come to Christ trusting his forgiveness and love to save and keep you. You will one day see him coming and confess him as Lord and King. You can do it now and become his child—or in his coming to be condemned. God calls you to come now!